*Jani Meier*

# OPEN TO CHANGE

# OPEN TO CHANGE

## David C. McCasland

This book is designed for your personal reading pleasure and profit. It is also designed for group study. A leader's guide with helps and hints for teachers and visual aids (Victor Multiuse Transparency Masters) is available from your local bookstore or from the publisher.

**VICTOR BOOKS**

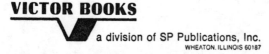

a division of SP Publications, Inc.
WHEATON. ILLINOIS 60187

*Offices also in* Fullerton, California • Whitby, Ontario, Canada • Amersham-on-the-Hill, Bucks, England

Unless otherwise noted, Scripture quotations are taken from the Holy Bible: *New International Version,* © 1978 by The New York International Bible Society. Used by permission of Zondervan Bible Publishers. Other quotations are from the King James Version (KJV), and *The New Testament in Modern English* (PH), © J.B. Phillips 1958, The Macmillan Company. Used by permission.

Recommended Dewey Decimal Classification: 248.1
   Suggested Subject Heading: Christian Life

Library of Congress Catalog Card Number: 80-52906
ISBN: 0–88207–258–7

VICTOR BOOKS
A division of SP Publications, Inc.
P.O. Box 1825 ● Wheaton, Illinois 60187

To the memory of my parents
Clyde and Pansy McCasland
Two people whose lives made a difference.

# Contents

# 1
# Consideration of Change

Several weeks ago at a luncheon in Denver, a man at a table near me collapsed to the floor in the throes of a heart attack. Over the public address system, a frantic voice asked if there was a doctor in the crowd of 400 people. There was none. The hotel house doctor was summoned and a man at our table who knew CPR techniques excused himself to see if he could help. The sound of the stricken man's groans and labored breathing could be heard throughout the room as people numbly turned back to their tables.

As I finished my cake and coffee and talked with the man next to me, the incongruity of the situation suddenly hit me. Here I was quietly finishing my dessert while a man was dying not 30 feet away from me. The feeling of helplessness was overpowering. He was either going to get better or die and there was nothing I could do about it. Nothing I did would alter things one way or another. The room silently screamed for a trained physician to move in, take charge, and turn the situation around. It never happened. By the time the ambulance arrived, the man was dead where he had fallen.

TURN IT AROUND! CHANGE IT! That's the challenge each of us faces in a hundred ways every day. Make a loser into a winner, an enemy into a friend, a dead group into a dynamic force, a sinner into a saint. Turn things around.

But in the face of that challenge, we are often frustrated with our inability to bring about the changes we seek. We may begin with enthusiasm, slow down with obstacles and failure, and end with resignation. "I tried to do something about it, but no one wanted my help—so I'll never try again," we say.

It's encouraging, however, to realize that Moses experienced a similar progression in his life. Enthusiasm, failure, and resignation. The beauty of Moses' story is that it doesn't end with resignation, but goes on to include the call of God which drew him out of obscurity and returned him to an arena of change he had walked from in defeat 40 years before. The experience of this man is a vast mine filled with valuable principles for people struggling to become God's agents of change in the 20th century.

Best of all, Moses' life isn't a Cinderella story. It's not an account of a quick move from everything wrong to everything right. Moses never ceased to struggle and learn in his relationship with God and in his role as an agent of change. He kept on making mistakes, learning, battling discouragement and opposition—just like we do. But he did it in an intimate, face to face relationship with God that took him over seemingly insurmountable obstacles.

## The Nature of Change

Let's be honest about change and our relationship to it. Nothing remains the same. Change is happening around and to us all the time, whether we choose to become involved in it or not. Some observers say that in the last 100 years, change itself has changed. No longer slow and methodical, it has become more rapid, and its effects on us more profound than ever before.

When Neil Armstrong set foot on the lunar surface, it ushered in a new age of thinking, centered in the seemingly limitless possibilities of human effort. Even advertisers were quick to pick up this line of reasoning. One popular TV commercial featured a man who lamented, "If they can send a man to the moon, why can't they make a decaffeinated coffee with real coffee taste?"

During the turbulent 1960s, a sudden and profound shift in attitudes rocked many countries. Primarily, this shift involved people's attitudes in these areas:

- A change from elder to youth orientation
- A change from postponed gratification to instant gratification
- A decline in the Puritan ethic
- A rise of the theology of pleasure: "If it feels good, do it."
- A change from sexual chastity to sexual freedom
- A loss of respect for government and all authority

To many despairing people, our world seems technologically, economically, and socially out of control. Prices are going up, morals are going down, and any efforts to counter these trends seem to be merely "spitting against the wind."

But as Christians, we follow and co-labor with the greatest Change Agent of history—Jesus Christ. Historian Will Durant believes that Christ is the Person who has the greatest continuing influence on Western civilization today. Jesus, the One who came as a servant, a washer of feet, and a sacrifice, secured our righteousness before God. And He has called us to follow Him, to go and make disciples among all nations. The Great Commission is our call to work for change.

We have opportunities to work for the most far-reaching changes possible in our world—the transformation of people from the inside out. The good news of Christ has always been a message of change. "Therefore, if anyone is in Christ, he is a new creation; the old has gone, the new has come!" (2 Cor. 5:17)

## How Do We Start?

How do we decide where to begin? Which changes are really worth working for? Again and again, we ask ourselves: *What difference has it made that I have lived on this earth? What is the net effect of all the days I've worked, petitions I've signed, children I've cared for, money I've made, votes I've cast, people I've known?*

Several years ago, a keen young man left a lucrative teaching position at a large, midwestern university to join the faculty of a small Christian college. As one of the top secular marketing men in the United States, he found that the changes he was working for didn't measure up to what he believed God wanted him to pursue. He summed up his decision by saying: "I decided I wanted to give the best years of my life to something

more than teaching bright young men and women how to sell tooth-
paste.'' Today, he is training people to function as Christian change
agents in communications, politics, business, education, and a host of
other areas.

What will it take to outlive ourselves in terms of continuing influence?
To make a lasting impact on a world that seems bent on swallowing up
our lives in anonymity? Here we encounter an unusual approach for
God's agents of change:

> Whoever wants to become great among you must be your
> servant, and whoever wants to be first must be slave of all. For
> even the Son of Man did not come to be served, but to serve,
> and to give His life as a ransom for many (Mark 10:43-44).

> The world and its desires pass away, but the man who does the
> will of God lives forever (1 John 2:17).

> Then He said to them all: ''If anyone would come after Me, he
> must deny himself and take up his cross daily and follow Me.
> For whoever wants to save his life will lose it, but whoever
> loses his life for Me will save it. What good is it for a man to
> gain the whole world, and yet lose or forfeit his very self? If
> anyone is ashamed of Me and My words, the Son of Man will
> be ashamed of him when He comes in His glory and in the
> glory of the Father and of the holy angels'' (Luke 9:23-26).

In a world that admires ''movers and shakers,'' God calls us to be
givers and helpers. We function as leaders who serve and as winners who
lose.

As Christian agents of change, we must reckon with the truth that God
has called us to work toward His goals, and has commissioned us to use
His methods in order to achieve them. In this modern, computerized
world, the greatest guidebook for agents of spiritual change is still the
Bible. It tells us about God's goals and His methods. Do we dare believe
that the Bible can and will guide us as we seek to become partners with
God, as we work for change in a world that desperately needs it, yet
viciously resists it? Dare we not believe it?

# Barriers to Change

Let's look at some obstacles that keep us from getting on with the job. What are the attitudes and feelings that hinder us from working effectively for change? Consider the following:

*We often feel disqualified to work in certain areas because of past mistakes and failures.* A divorced man told me recently, "I'm confused. I don't really know what kind of a ministry I can have and where God can use me. I feel like I can sing in the choir, but I don't feel like I can serve Communion. Can I ever teach the Bible again? How do I figure it out?"

Moses committed murder and became an exile from Egypt. How could God ever use him to bring about change for a people whose slavery and oppression had moved him to forceful, yet disastrous action? Do you feel disqualified from certain areas of service?

*We avoid areas where we have failed in the past.* I spent four years working with junior high students who hated school. School for them had been one failure after another since they started kindergarten. By junior high, they began taking measures to avoid it—truancy, classroom disruption, and dropping out when they reached age 16.

Most of us drop involvements where we consistently fail. Are there areas in which you have tried to bring about change in the past, only to fail miserably? How many times? What if God wants you to go back and try again?

*We tend to work only for those things which we think we have a good chance of achieving.* We need to set realistic goals, because lofty, nebulous objectives lead to frustration and abandoned efforts. But many times we refuse to aim high and risk failure. Thus, we never enter arenas of change where there are greater opportunities for Christ.

Management expert Peter Drucker, in his book *The Effective Executive*, says, "Courage rather than analysis dictates the truly important rules for identifying priorities: Pick the future as against the past; focus on opportunity rather than on problems; choose your own direction—rather than climb on the bandwagon; and aim high, aim for something that will make a difference, rather than for something that is 'safe' and easy to do" (Harper and Row, p. 111). Are we willing to dream a bit? And are we willing to set priorities that will move us toward making those dreams a reality?

*We get frustrated and discouraged easily.* Frustration comes when our efforts fail to bring about the desired results. Our level of frustration is directly related to the importance we attach to each change. Usually, the more important a change, the more difficult it is to bring it about—and the more frustrated we feel when it doesn't happen.

It is relatively easy for most people to change a light bulb, a tire, or a diaper. It takes a little more effort to change weekend plans, work schedules, or our own attitudes about something. When it comes to changing our spouse's mind, a company policy, or our child's attitude, we're talking about internal changes that require a lot of hard work. In these areas, we may feel highly frustrated—especially when our efforts at change don't succeed.

If our frustration level gets high enough, we may walk out of the situation as a final protest. Perhaps unconsciously we hope that our leaving will accomplish what our presence couldn't. Every day people walk away from jobs, marriages, children, churches, friends, and organizations as a final shout of protest against situations and people who wouldn't change.

Our discouragement can be the result of our confusing visibility and usefulness. When no one knows or appreciates what we are doing, when we feel obscure, unnoticed, and unnecessary, our will to continue reaches a low ebb.

*We often work from the notion that any method is valid as long as it accomplishes the desired goal.* I'll never forget, as a high school sophomore, my first big red "X" on a geometry problem. I got the right answer, but I used a wrong method.

"You've got to be kidding me," I protested. "As long as I get the right answer, what difference does it make how I get it?"

Our basketball coach, who also taught geometry, loomed over me with his red pencil poised to strike again and said, "McCasland, in geometry the means and the end are equally important. You've got to learn them both."

*We have the mistaken notion that as soon as we begin doing the right thing, our situation will immediately get better.* The assurance we have from God is that as we continue to do the right thing, He will strengthen and support us—even though the situation may *not* immediately get better. Things may get progressively worse for a long time before God finally makes them right.

*We are often unwilling to invest the amount of time necessary to accomplish deep, meaningful change.* Words such as patience, perseverance, long-suffering, endurance, and waiting fill the pages of Scripture. Yet our desire for instant success goads us to speed up processes, which by their very nature take a lot of time. We want to spray a light coat of oil over the swamp and declare the mosquito problem conquered instead of working toward drainage of the stagnant water and reclamation of the land. That takes time.

*We are too ready to abandon our efforts at change when they begin to threaten our personal success and well-being.* Rarely, it seems, do we embark on a project with an accurate knowledge of just what it will cost us in terms of time, energy, and money. In one sense, this may be good in that it overcomes our selfish tendencies which would hinder our even beginning. But involvement in significant change calls for a continuing evaluation of the cost and a renewed commitment, even when our efforts take more time than our original estimate.

Probably Moses had no idea what agonies of soul were in store for him as he undertook the deliverance of Israel. But his loyalty and dedication to God were exemplary. Even when the rebellious, complaining Israelites blamed him for all of their problems, Moses still sought God's wisdom and compassion to undergird him in fulfilling his commitment.

Even for us there will be days of ecstatic success, nights of lonely obscurity, and long afternoons of ordinariness. But as we allow God to change us, we will discover new horizons of usefulness.

## Volunteers for God

Most people are confronted each day with situations and people whom they would like to see changed. Some may feel that past failures have disqualified them from further significant service for God; others may feel that their present efforts go unnoticed and are ineffective; still others may find that change is taking much more effort and time than they had anticipated.

Christians should become involved in the world as agents of change in a variety of contexts—families, politics, community affairs, mass media, the arts, education, medicine, ethics, law, and many others. All of us should seek God's leading in how He wants to impact our world through us, in compassion, in caring, in service, and in love.

Major Walter Reed was the U.S. Army physician whose experiments and research led to the discovery of a cure for yellow fever. Reed received much recognition for his work, but he couldn't have done it without the help of a little-known army private named John Kissinger.

In 1900, Reed had reached a stalemate in his research. He had learned all he could from animals. But he felt he could never ask a human to volunteer for the needed experiments, which involved probable contraction of yellow fever and possible death.

When Private Kissinger learned of the need, he gave long and painstaking thought to the situation and the dangers involved. Finally, he volunteered himself to Dr. Reed by saying, "Sir, you can start on me."

There is nothing that brings us to the cutting edge of life more quickly than having the spirit of a volunteer. In becoming God's agents of change, we give our heavenly Father the go-ahead to perform His work in us and use us in the lives of others.

Perhaps, before going any farther, we might each want to pause and say to God, regarding His work of change in this world, "Sir, You can start on me."

# STUDY QUESTIONS

1. Of the attitudes and feelings which describe your hesitancy to work toward change, do any describe your feelings about yourself right now?

2. Since being God's agent of change involves His work in us and through us, (a) Which area of your own internal life do you find most in need of change? (b) In which area involving people and situations around you do you believe God most wants to use you to work toward change?

3. Read Ephesians 3:20-21. How do you feel this passage relates to the two areas you listed in question 2?

4. How do you tell the difference between having realistic expectations regarding change and being afraid to launch out in faith and take a risk?

5. What are your expectations for your reading and study of this book?

# 2
# Cultivated

As our 737 climbed high into the blue February morning, the Rocky Mountains quickly slipped away behind us. The splendor of the snow-capped peaks gradually gave way to the barren landscape of northern New Mexico and then to the high plateau country of west Texas. The area below us was a study in stark contrasts.

Dotted around the bleak and barren countryside were circles of green. Many times I had driven this route and noted from ground level the presence of these patches of winter wheat. But from 33,000 feet in the air, the contrast was striking. The green patches showed evidence of a master designer, a farmer who had painstakingly prepared the ground, cultivated it, planted it, and then watered it. Where there had been time spent on cultivation, there was life and the promise of new growth. Where no man had been, the land lay undisturbed, unproductive, a barren brown.

## God Cultivates Us

If you are a child of God by faith in Jesus Christ, God is at work in your life through His own unique process of cultivation. For people who desire to become God's agents of change, we must recognize this process of spiritual cultivation, realize its necessity, and be thankful that God uses every experience of our lives, good and bad, as He trains us. The

*American Heritage Dictionary* defines the word *cultivate* in the following ways: "to improve and prepare land for raising crops; to grow or tend, as a plant or crop; to form and refine, as by education."

If I were a parcel of land, I'd enjoy seeing my crops grow and flourish. There would be a great sense of worth and accomplishment during the harvest at seeing how I had been used to bring forth life-giving food. Then there would be the quiet sense of well-being and rest in lying fallow after the time of reaping.

But I wouldn't like to lie quietly basking in the sun while some farmer drove over me with a tractor and ripped me open with a plow. That would hurt too much!

"Hey, cut it out, will ya? Just scatter some seed over me and let's get on with it."

As if it wasn't enough to tear me up with a plow, he'd be back later with a disc to slice me up into smaller pieces.

"Give me a break! We did this last year, didn't we?"

But the farmer wouldn't give up on me yet. After the disc had done its work, the farmer would come back with a harrow and perhaps a roller to rake and smooth me. Only at that point would I be ready for planting and potential crop production.

## "But I've Got Problems!"

Many of us may hesitate to work toward changing a situation because we feel disqualified due to something in our past. Instead of seeing the past as part of God's cultivation process, we may see it as a time in which the landscape of our lives was sown with salt, inhibiting any future growth in terms of spiritual success. If our background includes failures, disappointments, and even difficulties over which we had no control, we may feel that our role must be one of passive acceptance rather than active work toward change.

Suppose Moses could appear today and analyze his own background before he answered God's call. I wonder what he would say. Would Moses' reasoning sound something like this?

"Talk about a terrible background—I had one. I was born into the middle of an oppressive political situation. My people had no Constitution or Bill of Rights. They were kept in subjugation by a powerful, ruling nation. They weren't even called second-class citizens. They were slaves.

"Read about it for yourself (see Ex. 1:8-14). The Egyptians worked my people ruthlessly. After Joseph died, the new king of Egypt tried to stop our population growth by forcing the people to throw their newborn sons into the river. By all rights, I never should have made it through infancy.

"I was nursed by my natural mother until weaned, then taken to Pharaoh's daughter where I became her son. I was an adopted child who was raised in a racially mixed family.

"Oh, I got a good education, but it wasn't one that could be considered godly. I was prepared for a role that I never assumed in life. As part of the royal family, I had too much money, too much time, and too many opportunities to do things I shouldn't have. Later on, I spent much of my life unlearning what my education in school and in the royal court had taught me.

"As I grew up, I became painfully aware of who my people were. Seeing their plight caused the greatest conflict of my life up to that point. I took matters into my own hands and ended up exiled, with nothing, absolutely nothing to show for the first 40 years of my life."

The diverse, often unfavorable aspects of Moses' background should encourage us as we consider God's marvelous ability to use every experience of our lives as part of His process of cultivation. Nothing in our lives is wasted.

## The Blame Game

Can you think of five things you wish had never happened to you? For most of us, that's not difficult. Young or old, it doesn't take long to recall five events that we wish had never occurred. What would you choose? The untimely death of someone close to you? A divorce or romantic heartbreak? Your relationship with your mother or father? A decision which you feel has adversely affected your life?

There is a tendency among some Christians to think: *If I were someone else, God could use me in a mighty way. But look at me. I'm not a professional athlete, a former drug addict, a glamor queen, a successful businessman, or a gifted speaker. I didn't have the right opportunities while growing up. I never went to college. No, my background just doesn't measure up.*

One danger of contemplating our backgrounds is that we may blame others too much for the way we are. In his thought-provoking book, *The Kink and I* (Victor, p. 210), Dr. James D. Mallory shares the following song by Anna Russell:

> I went to my psychiatrist
> To be psychoanalyzed,
> To find out why I killed the cat
> And blackened my wife's eyes.
>
> He put me on a downy couch
> To see what he could find,
> And this is what he dredged up
> From my subconscious mind:
>
> When I was one, my mommy hid
> My dolly in the trunk,
> And so it follows naturally,
> That I am always drunk.
>
> When I was two, I saw my father
> Kiss the maid one day,
> And that is why I suffer now—
> Kleptomania.
>
> When I was three, I suffered from
> Ambivalence toward my brothers,
> So it follows naturally,
> I poisoned all my lovers.
>
> I'm so glad that I have learned
> The lesson it has taught,
> That everything I do that's wrong
> Is someone else's fault!

# Give Your Past to God

As a young man making my first independent forays into the world, I can still remember my father's parting words each time I'd leave home: "If you need me, call me." My natural response to handling a difficulty beyond my ability would have been to call my dad. He wanted me to call and he wanted to help. In the same way, our heavenly Father wants us to come to Him with the tough circumstances and events of life—present and past.

Even if you are used to presenting today and tomorrow to God and asking for His help, your past often remains something with which you feel you must cope alone. Have you ever given your childhood to Christ? Have you given to Him those five things you wish had never happened to you? Have you asked Him to use those events in His process of building you into the person He wants you to be? What about your teenage years? Disappointing relationships? Failures in things that were vitally important to you?

God uses people who are humble: "God opposes the proud but gives grace to the humble. Humble yourselves, therefore, under God's mighty hand, that He may lift you up in due time" (1 Peter 5:5-6). Most of us don't develop humility through our successes. We learn humility through experiences that show us exactly who we are and who God is. Humility is not a bowed head, broken-spirit attitude in which we tell ourselves how horrible we are. True humility is simply understanding who God is and who we are. It means remembering where we have come from and where God is taking us.

God also uses people who depend on Him as His change agents. In Psalm 50, God indicates what He desires on the part of those who are committed to serving Him. Here is one dimension of that relationship: "Call upon Me in the day of trouble; I will deliver you, and you will honor Me" (v. 15).

W. T. Sleeper wrote these beautiful words:

> Out of my bondage, sorrow and night,
> Jesus, I come. Jesus, I come.
> Into Thy freedom, gladness, and light,
> Jesus I come to Thee.

# God's Perspective of the Past

In the light of God's cultivation process in our lives, past events that have seemed to be blights and blemishes can be seen in a new way.

God has constructed some beautiful lives out of what appeared to be only the rubble of the past. On October 31, 1896, a baby was born to an unwed 13-year-old girl in the bleak west end section of Chester, Pennsylvania. The baby had been conceived at knife-point through forcible rape. Though the baby was bounced around from one shanty to another in the slums of Philadelphia, she survived, grew, and began to sing. Mostly, she sang the blues because that was what she knew.

She became a star and nobody could sing "Stormy Weather" like Ethel Waters could. At the age of 61, Ethel gave her life to Christ and her songs reflected the change.

"When I found Jesus," Ethel once said, "I stopped singing the song 'Stormy Weather,' which I had made world-famous. When I sang that song, my life was like that. But it isn't anymore. Now my life is reflected in the songs I sing about God's love. If I get a heart attack, I'm not going to call on 'Stormy Weather,' I'm going to call on my Jesus" (Twila Knaack, *Ethel Waters—I Touched a Sparrow*, Word, p. 19).

Ethel Waters ministered to millions of people through her singing. "I sing because I'm happy, I sing because I'm free. For His eye is on the sparrow, and I know He watches me." When she made Christ the Lord of her life, He began to make something beautiful of her past.

Recently I admired a small, framed plaque of an antique Rolls-Royce touring car, hung on a wall in a successful businessman's office. As I examined the plaque in detail, I was startled as I realized the materials from which the car had been made. There were paper clips, thumbtacks, old clock gears, brads, wires, and safety pins. They were blended so artistically that the total effect was one of beauty, quality, and taste. It struck me as a vivid illustration of what God can do with the events of our lives when we make Him the Master Architect and Builder. A lot of the materials and experiences we may see as worthless, He blends together into a creation of beauty and usefulness.

It helps to remember that the products of God's cultivation are unique persons for unique ministries. This isn't an assembly line process where everything comes out the same at the end. While God has called and uniquely used Mother Teresa to minister to the poorest of the poor in India, He has also used men like the late Art DeMoss to reach out to many of the world's wealthy in the name of Christ.

God comforts us "in all our troubles, so that we can comfort those in any trouble with the comfort we ourselves have received from God" (2 Cor. 1:4). Your unique ministry as an agent of change will grow out of God's cultivation of you through your personal experiences and background. God's creativity and imagination in preparing you for the harvest field free you from the necessity of comparing yourself with other people. It also enables you to thank Him for the things He has given you to do.

In the kingdom of God, no one is disqualified from service because of adverse background or previous failure. In fact, these are generally common characteristics of people in the process of cultivation. The challenge is to believe that God can and will take your past and begin to build something beautiful out of it.

"I waited patiently for the Lord; He turned to me and heard my cry. He lifted me out of the slimy pit, out of the mud and mire; He set my feet on a rock and gave me a firm place to stand. He put a new song in my mouth, a hymn of praise to our God. Many will see and fear and put their trust in the Lord" (Ps. 40:1-3). " 'For I know the plans I have for you,' delcares the Lord, 'plans to prosper you and not to harm you, plans to give you hope and a future' " (Jer. 29:11).

# STUDY QUESTIONS

1. What five unfavorable things might Moses have chosen to eliminate from his life?

2. How much less prepared for God's work would he have been if he hadn't experienced those five things?

3. What makes the difference between difficult past experiences becoming stumbling blocks or stepping-stones?

4. How would you explain to another person the process you should follow in bringing your past to God and asking Him to use it as part of His cultivation of your life? How does the truth of 1 John 1:9 fit into your explanation?

5. Is there any past event of your life which you feel God could never

use for His glory? Read again Psalm 40:1-3 and Jeremiah 29:11. What would it take to convince you that this is within the realm of possibility for you?

# 3
# Captivated

History is filled with examples of men and women who have brought about significant changes because they became captivated by causes greater than themselves. Yet history also gives numerous accounts of misguided individuals who were captivated by worthy causes but used deplorable methods to reach their goals. While captivation seems to be a necessary motivational factor, it is also an area of potential danger for a Christian agent of change.

Basically, we face the danger of becoming captivated by a *cause* instead of being captivated by the Person of *Jesus Christ*. When we give ourselves merely to a cause, we have yielded our allegiance to something less than God Himself. The writer to the Hebrews urges us to run with perseverance the race marked out for us, with our eyes fixed on Jesus, the Author and Perfecter of our faith (Heb. 12:2). When we are committed to a cause instead of to Christ, misdirection, disorientation, frustration, and failure are the inevitable results.

I believe that four words—observation, indignation, supplication, and intervention—describe a progression that should characterize our lives.

## Observation
One day, Moses went out to where his own people were and watched them at their hard labor (Ex. 2:11). Like Moses, each of us is confronted

every day with need and injustice. In one country people are starving, while people in another country shell out $11 million for a popular diet book. We live and work with people whose needs range from an effective mouthwash to a cure for terminal cancer. Our lives are spent observing others. Perhaps as a psychological survival technique, we have learned to screen out even the most troublesome impressions when they threaten to disrupt the order of our lives.

This was probably not the first time Moses had observed the Hebrews at their hard labor. No doubt he had been aware of this situation for many years. For "Moses was educated in all the wisdom of the Egyptians" (Acts 7:22). He knew all the reasons behind keeping the Hebrews in subjection. They were essential to the Egyptian economy. Their hardship supported his lifestyle. With no restraints, they would have posed a threat to his very way of life.

## Indignation

But something different happened that day as Moses observed. He saw an Egyptian beating a Hebrew, *one of his own people* (Ex. 2:11-12). Moses' involvement in the situation suddenly moved from the intellectual to the emotional. One of his people was suffering injustice and Moses was gripped by the inequity of it all. In addition to seeing, he began feeling.

Our sense of indignation may not be as strong as Moses'. But it is essential for motivating us to try and change something. Until we begin to feel strongly, we probably won't be moved to action. And herein is a danger: the stronger our emotional reaction to a need, the more likely we are to take immediate action. Just as Moses did, we may skip the all-important step of going to God in prayer.

## Supplication

Moses found it unnecessary to consult with God on this matter. The results of his failure to do so are evident. In his anger, Moses killed an Egyptian. There was nothing wrong with Moses' sense of morality or his willingness to take action. The missing ingredient was a conversation with God.

By taking action on his own, Moses probably short-circuited the entire process of deliverance for Israel. He thrust himself into a learning cycle that took him from the power circles of Egypt to the desert of Midian. But during the next 40 years, he learned the part that this desert experience played in the process of working toward change.

Consider for a moment the scriptural account of another agent of change who knew the power of prayer. Nehemiah received bad news about his countrymen: "Those who survived the Exile and are back in the province are in great trouble and disgrace. The wall of Jerusalem is broken down, and its gates have burned with fire" (Neh. 1:3). Emotionally moved, Nehemiah sat down and wept. Then, "For some days [he] mourned and fasted and prayed before the God of heaven" (1:4). Instead of jumping on his camel and riding off in all four directions at once, Nehemiah brought the need before Almighty God and sought His direction. Nehemiah's success in rebuilding the walls of Jerusalem was directly related to his act of prayer before taking action.

Prayer focuses our attention beyond the need or the cause to the One we serve, the One whose directions we follow, the One who can empower us to work toward His changes in His ways.

Moses should have fallen to his knees in prayer before God. But instead he glanced around to see if he could get away with what he had in mind. In working toward spiritual change, many Christians are like Moses. They look around to see what *they* want to do instead of humbly approaching God and asking, "Lord, what do You want? How do You want me to do it?"

## Intervention

For Christian agents of change, *the end does not justify the means*. God has set before us goals of reconciling people to Him and standing against injustice and evil. But He has also given us principles to follow as we go about doing these things. We are not free to use any means to gain the desired end.

Our world is heavily committed to *pragmatism,* which can be loosely defined as "whatever works." As a junior high English teacher, I was intrigued by students' reactions to spelling tests. When I would show students the correct way to spell a word, they would almost always respond by saying, "Well, whatever." The point of spelling and grammar is that "whatever," if taken far enough, will lead to linguistic chaos.

It's hard enough for someone from New York to communicate with someone from Texas, without turning the country loose to spell words and arrange them in sentences as they please.

It seems that one difficulty in working for change, even as Christians, is that we approach it as an art rather than as a science. Let me explain. Language is an art. You can go to the grocery store, hand the clerk a bill, and say, "I don't got no change." The clerk will understand what you mean and probably not correct your grammar. Language can be understood even when it's incorrect.

But mathematics is a science. If you go to the grocery store, pass through the check-out counter with $37.86 worth of goods, and hand the clerk only $10 as payment—you will have a problem. In a science, the method and the outcome are inseparably linked. You cannot achieve the desired end without following the proper method.

The Bible shows us God's guidelines for bringing about changes. Obviously, we are not free to kill, lie, steal, or cheat to bring people to faith in Christ. But in the grip of an emotional reaction to a need, it is easy to forget to compare our methods to God's standard.

At first, it may seem that Moses' killing of the Egyptian passed the test of pragmatism. It worked—at least for 24 hours. But for a method to be correct, it must stand the test of time—and eternity.

Christ's interaction with His disciples exposes our own tendency to use wrong methods as we try to bring about change. Consider these instances:

- Five thousand people needed something to eat. The disciples said: "Send the crowds away" (Matt. 14:15).
- A Samaritan village refused to welcome Jesus. The disciples said: "Lord, do You want us to call fire down from heaven to destroy them?" (Luke 9:54)
- Blind Bartimaeus shouted, " 'Jesus, Son of David, have mercy on me!' Many rebuked him and told him to be quiet" (Mark 10:47-48).

"Send them away, burn the village, quiet that blind man!" In the mirror of Scripture, we see our own need to have our intervention first tempered and then directed through prayer and Bible study.

# Captivation

Yes, Moses was captivated. But he settled for devotion to a cause in his earliest efforts at change. Without his focus on God Himself, Moses saw the cause out of perspective and got tangled in a web of difficulties. We too face problems similar to Moses' when we are captivated only by a cause.

Consider the following dangers in being captivated only by a cause:

(1) A cause can easily become an obsession. We all know people who have become consumed by a cause to the detriment of their families, their jobs, and even their own health. A spiritual agent of change should walk a line of tension between dedication and obsession.

(2) Captivation by a cause can lead to fringe efforts which are only remotely related to our calling as Christians. Usually, only the people involved can tell when they are out of balance in a certain situation. If devotion to a particular cause leads us to neglect our own personal time with God through prayer and Bible reading, then perhaps our energies are being misdirected. We should rearrange our priorities so that our most important relationships don't suffer. We must not forget either about the people around us who need the Saviour.

(3) Captivation by a cause can lead to reactionary tactics. When Moses responded to injustice against the Hebrews, he used the wrong method and short-circuited his ability to do something positive. A change agent must constantly evaluate his methods in light of the Scriptures.

Test your methods against these words: "Do not let any unwholesome talk come out of your mouths, but only what is helpful for building others up according to their needs, that it may benefit those who listen. And do not grieve the Holy Spirit of God, with whom you were sealed for the day of redemption. Get rid of all bitterness, rage and anger, brawling and slander, along with every form of malice. Be kind and compassionate to one another, forgiving each other, just as in Christ, God forgave you" (Eph. 4:29-32).

(4) Captivation by a cause often leads to a feeling of exclusiveness. When we have little use for people who don't beat the same drum or ride the same hobby horse as we, then we cut ourselves off from others.

Our world is fragmented into groups who have little use for those who disagree with them. Recently, the pilot of a commercial jet had to land

and eject several passengers who had gotten into a fight over what was and wasn't the non-smoking section of the aircraft.

While we tend toward exclusivity in our humanity, Jesus Christ was the most *inclusive* Person who ever lived. He reached out and loved those who didn't agree with Him, those who weren't like Him, and even those who hated Him. When we are captivated by Christ, we won't let our causes separate us from a world in need.

During the last week of my mother's life, I was privileged to spend a lot of time with her in the hospital. For many silent hours she was comatose, yet clinging tenaciously to life. But one afternoon, only a few days before she died, she was unusually alert. We spent several hours talking together.

At one point, she mentioned how glad she was that I had had so many opportunities during my life to study the Bible. There in the hospital room, I was painfully aware that I possessed a great deal of information about God and the Bible. Yet those great truths and the Person behind them did not have a grip on my life.

My tears flowed freely as I told Mother about my spiritual need. My heart's desire was that Jesus Christ would get hold of me—that in a deep, new way, God's Word would grip my life. Sitting beside my mother, whom I loved dearly and whose life was ending, I made a discovery. I realized that the direction of my life would be determined, not by what I had a grip on, but by who had a grip on me.

The Apostle Paul expressed the aim of his life by saying, "I press on to take hold of that for which Christ Jesus took hold of me" (Phil. 3:12). Our devotion to Christ can be expressed through our participation in a variety of causes. Yet the cause should never captivate our allegiance. That is to be reserved for the One who died and rose again that we might be delivered from our slavery to sin. We have been delivered so that we might represent the Deliverer.

Have you been gripped by the love of Jesus Christ for you? Are you captured and captivated by this God who became a man and experienced the hunger, tiredness, loneliness, and pain of living and dying?

Moses finally met God late in life in a burning bush. There his cause and his Captivator were combined to lead him out of failure into a partnership that called a nation out of bondage into God's service.

# STUDY QUESTIONS

1. What example can you give from your own experience in which you or someone you know has worked for the right goal, using the wrong method?

2. In your own experience, would you say you too easily become involved in working toward change, or that you are too reticent when it comes to involvement in causes? What do you feel is the key to achieving balance?

3. Have you ever studied the life of Christ as a perfect example of someone who blended God's methods and goals in living on this earth? Consider the alternatives Jesus used when the disciples suggested sending the hungry people away, burning the village, and quieting the blind man.

4. Which of the four dangers of being captivated only by a cause is the one to which you are most susceptible?

5. Read Nehemiah's prayer (Neh. 1:4-11). Analyze what he said to God, what he asked for, and what he did as a result of his prayer. How is his prayer a sound example to us as we pray for change?

# 4
# Cast Aside

In Moses' first attempt at changing the oppressive situation of his own people, he was disqualified by a false start. He was barely out of the starting blocks when his participation in the race came to a screeching halt. And what a tragedy!

Who was better qualified than Moses? He knew both sides of the issue. He was educated in all the wisdom of the Egyptians and was powerful in speech and action (Acts 7:22). He had recognized the Hebrews as his own people and had chosen to identify with them.

There was even an act of faith involved here: "By faith, Moses, when he had grown up, refused to be known as the son of Pharaoh's daughter. He chose to be mistreated along with the people of God rather than to enjoy the pleasures of sin for a short time" (Heb. 11:24-25). But Moses was not yet the man whom God could use to change the plight of the Hebrews. Neither was the time ripe for action. God had something in mind far beyond Moses' wildest dreams. It was necessary for Moses to face adversity so that he could learn to know and depend on God.

## Moses' Attempt at Deliverance

When Moses killed the Egyptian, it was—in some ways—a daring act of courage. A severe penalty (probably death) awaited any person, particularly a Hebrew, who rose up in violence against one of the Egyptian taskmasters. Moses made an impressive move that should have shown the Hebrews that he was a man of action—ready to move, ready to turn their oppressive situation around. Unfortunately, it neither impressed the Hebrews nor changed their situation.

Impulsively, Moses had attacked the external force of oppression. Perhaps he didn't realize that there was an internal issue that needed to be dealt with as well. The Hebrew "organization" had problems both within and without. The next day, Moses encountered the internal issue when he came upon two Hebrews fighting with each other. When he asked the one in the wrong, "Why are you hitting your fellow Hebrew?" he received a devastating response.

"Who made you ruler and judge over us?" the Hebrew asked (Ex. 2:14). Moses had wrongly assumed that he (Moses) was the one to solve the problem. But his Hebrew brother told Moses to mind his own business and leave him alone. The two who argued didn't feel that Moses had any right to question their behavior—much less to deal with the internal problems of the people.

Next, the combative Hebrew, who was "in the wrong" (v. 13), threw Moses' act of violence right in his face. "Are you thinking of killing me as you killed the Egyptian?" (v. 14) Here was the repudiation of Moses' method of dealing with the oppressors.

Moses had failed on two counts: first in his effort to stand up against the Egyptian taskmasters; and second, in his effort to reconcile the fighting internal factions among the Hebrews themselves.

## Sensing God's Timing

Several months ago I made extensive plans for a business trip which hinged on the final production of a promotional videotape. The day before the tape went into final production, I felt pretty nervous. My wife and I paused to pray about the situation, asking for God's guidance and direction. That afternoon, the local television station where I was to produce the tape cancelled my production session for that evening. No other time would be available between then and the day I was scheduled to leave. I had to cancel the business trip.

Later, I complained about the cancellation of the trip, the unfairness of the local station, and all the work it would take to set things up again. It seemed that things had fallen apart in my hands. In the middle of my gripe session, my wife confronted me with two questions:

"Did we pray about the tape and the trip?"

"Well, I guess we did."

"Did we ask God to direct you?"

"Yeah, but . . ."

"Then we have to trust that this is part of His direction and thank Him for it. All you know is that you didn't get your tape finished. God may have a lot of other reasons He didn't want you to go right now."

Thank God for a closed door? It struck me as odd. I can get so fired up and thankful when God opens a door in my life. But it bothers me when He closes one. As I seek God's leadership and timing, I should get just as excited about the doors He closes as I do about the doors He opens. They're both part of His work.

Sensing God's timing has always been somewhat of a mystery to me. But this is not a game of spiritual hide and seek in which we try to discover God's plan and He tries to hide it from us. Rather it is a process in which God delights to involve and lead us.

In chapter 3 we saw the need for prayer as a necessary step in our process of working toward change. As we pray, we should simply ask, "Lord, is this the right time to move in this area?" It is God's pleasure to guide and direct us in response to our dependence on Him.

Throughout Scripture, we are reminded that God takes action when the time is right. Christ was born "in the fullness of time" (Gal. 4:4). "When the times will have reached their fulfillment—to bring all things in heaven and on earth together under one head, even Christ" (Eph. 1:10). Solomon in his wisdom wrote, "There is a time for everything" (Ecc. 3:1). In some cases, our failure to bring about the change we desire can be traced directly to our failure to follow God's timing.

In Stephen's testimony of the history of Israel, he said: "Moses thought that his own people would realize that God was using him to rescue them, but they did not" (Acts 7:25). Why didn't the Hebrews realize that God was using Moses to rescue them? Primarily because God *was not* using Moses—at least not at that time.

"Since we live by the Spirit, let us keep in step with the Spirit" (Gal. 5:25). Discovering God's timing for change involves pausing to ask for

His direction. Then we should thank Him whether He says go ahead, wait, or forget it.

## Facing Up to Failure

As we consider working toward a change, we should ask ourselves if we're ready to be used to make the change. Obviously Moses was not ready to be God's instrument of change in his situation. While it is difficult to accurately assess our preparation for the task at hand, we can submit ourselves to God and cooperate as He molds us into useful servants.

Moses failed. Yet his failure, and ours, place us among a great company of people who have experienced the terrible feeling of having tried and fallen short. Consider the following examples of three of the most respected figures of American history:

- At 22, he failed in business. The next year, he ran for the legislature and was defeated. At 24, he again failed in business. After his election to the legislature, his sweetheart died. During the next 20 years, he was twice defeated for Congress, twice defeated for the Senate, and once defeated for Vice-President. At the age of 51, Abraham Lincoln was elected President of the United States.
- Thomas Edison was sent home from school because his teacher said he was too stupid to learn.
- Albert Einstein was expelled from school at the age of 15 because he showed no interest in his studies. He later failed the entrance exam to Zurich Polytechnic.

Failure is common in human experience. Yet, the realization that others have failed often doesn't alleviate our pain and anguish when we fail. Misery may love company, but it doesn't find much encouragement in it. The value of seeing others' failures lies in seeing how they overcame their defeats and moved back toward useful lives.

There are many accounts of heroic failures in the Bible. But the Scriptures take us beyond the point of despair in those peoples' lives.

- David was guilty of adultery and murder, yet after his repentance,

God used him. He is referred to as a man after God's own heart (Acts 13:22).

- Saul of Tarsus was proud, arrogant, and the chief persecutor of Christians. When he encountered Christ on the road to Damascus, he fell to his knees asking, "Lord, what will You have me to do?" (Acts 9:6, KJV) God then used Paul to spread the message of Christ throughout the Mediterranean world.

- Peter suffered during the early years of his discipleship from a recurring case of foot-in-mouth disease. He was always saying the wrong thing. He tried to save Jesus with a sword, but later swore that he had never known the Lord. He wept bitter tears of repentance and became the first voice of the church at Pentecost.

Failure tells us to quit, forget it, hang it up, and resign ourselves to living a second-class life because of what we have done.

I firmly believe that as Moses fled Egypt, his dominant feeling was not fear, but one of resignation. He was resigned to the fact that his effort at change had failed miserably. Not only had he failed, but he had done it in such a way that he had apparently spoiled any chances for future success in this endeavor. Moses must have felt that he had been not merely penalized, but thrown out of the game. And it was a long walk to the showers in Midian.

## An Act of Faith

It's easy for us to think that Moses was running away from his troubles in Egypt. But the writer of the Book of Hebrews gives an interesting insight into Moses' situation. "By faith he left Egypt, not fearing the king's anger; he persevered because he saw Him who is invisible" (Heb. 11:27). At first glance, we might conclude that this refers to the time when Moses led the nation of Israel out of Egypt at the beginning of the Exodus. But a careful examination of the context and chronology of this passage leads me to a different conclusion.

When Moses left Egypt for his exile in Midian, he did it by faith. In Hebrews 11:4-31, all the acts of faith are mentioned in chronological order. There is no deviation from this pattern. Note the record of Moses' life in Hebrews 11:

By faith, Moses' parents hid him (v. 23).
By faith, Moses, when he had grown up, refused to be known as the son of Pharaoh's daughter (v. 24).
By faith, he left Egypt, not fearing the king's anger (v. 27).
By faith, he kept the Passover and the sprinkling of blood, so that the destroyer of the firstborn would not touch the firstborn of Israel (v. 28).
By faith, the people passed through the Red Sea (v. 29).

We know that Moses left Egypt twice, once for exile in Midian and again as the leader of the Israelites. The observance of the Passover and the sprinkling of blood occurred while Israel was still in Egypt, on the last night before they left. Therefore, according to the chronology of this passage, it seems that Moses' act of faith in leaving Egypt refers to his journey into exile.

But how could that be an act of faith? Don't we read that Moses was afraid that his act of violence had become known? (Ex. 2:14-15) That Pharaoh tried to kill him and that he fled from Pharaoh? How can we reconcile the apparently contradictory passages describing Moses' first exit from Egypt?

Perhaps you have noticed that other New Testament passages seem overly favorable to Old Testament characters in light of their actions. Of Abraham we read, "He did not waver through unbelief regarding the promise of God" (Rom. 4:20). He didn't? When he went down to Egypt to escape the famine? When he referred to his wife, Sarah, as his sister? When he fathered a child through Hagar?

Peter wrote that Lot was a righteous man who was distressed by the filthy lives of lawless men (2 Peter 2:7). Righteous Lot? The one who lived in Sodom? Whose family was caught in the grip of that decadent society? Who argued with God about where to go to escape the destruction to come?

These seeming contradictions point us to a God who sees inside us, down deep to our heart attitudes that transcend the actions and events of the moment. Those who were commended for their faith went through great struggles during their spiritual development.

That spark of faith in Moses' life was buried under a deep layer of resignation. We read that "Moses fled from Pharaoh and went to *live* in Midian" (Ex. 2:15). He wasn't dropping in for a visit, or for a few months until things cooled off back home. He had come to stay.

## God's Forgiveness

Is there something in your life which you feel has disqualified you from serving God? What kind of failure has brought you to the place of resignation? Have you been dishonest in your business dealings, been unfaithful to your spouse, lost your temper and slammed the door on a relationship, committed a crime, surrendered to alcohol or drug addiction?

Or perhaps your resignation comes from a continuing series of failures—little things you said you would never do again, but time after time have dragged you down so that you've withdrawn from the battle saying, "What's the use?"

Your spiritual exile may be one of withdrawal, undergirded by your constant repeating of "If only I had" or "If only I hadn't." But that spark of faith is still alive in your heart—the one that was kindled when you committed your life to Jesus Christ. Like Moses, perhaps you feel that you haven't abandoned God. Maybe you feel that He has abandoned you from the standpoint of including you in His service as you had once dreamed. Moses' experience teaches us that with God, there is always another chance.

In his book *Future Shock* (Random House), Alvin Toffler called modern America the "throwaway society" and made us aware of the number of items which are designed to be used and discarded. Ball-point pens, plastic lighters, bottles, and cans go from hand to trash can. But now when fuel and raw materials are no longer cheap or plentiful, our throwaway society is coming to an end. The word *recycle* which didn't even appear in the 1960 edition of *Webster's New Collegiate Dictionary* is now a household word.

To my knowledge, the word *recycle* never appears in the Bible—but the concept is there. The idea is applied not to things, but to people. While we tend to write others and ourselves off as failures, God sees what we can become when we respond in simple faith to Him.

"God, I tried and failed. I've failed more than once. But if You can pick me up, hold me, and strengthen me, I'll try again." Remember, there are no throwaways in God's economy.

On the basis of biblical evidence, we see that no one is ever disqualified from God's service simply on the basis of past failures. Disqualification results from an unwillingness to come to God in repentance and humility and ask His forgiveness.

Though Moses felt cast aside, he had entered the Lord's school of discipline and humility. Years later he was allowed to fulfill the dream he had seemingly forfeited by taking matters into his own hands.

> Blessed is the man You discipline, O Lord, the man You teach
> from Your Law; You grant him relief from days of trouble, till
> a pit is dug for the wicked. For the Lord will not reject [cast off]
> His people; He will never forsake His inheritance.
>
> Psalm 94:12-14

# STUDY QUESTIONS

1. Is there a difference in your reaction to "open doors" and "closed doors" from God? How would seeing both of these as His work change your attitude?

2. Search your past and see if you can recognize some things you thought were failures, but which God has turned into successes. Is there a situation in which you need to ask God to do the same thing today?

3. What do you think Moses learned from his experience of killing the Egyptian and being rejected by the Hebrews?

4. What do you feel is the key for a Christian in turning failure into success?

# 5
# Curtailed

Moses went from the pinnacle in Egypt to the pits in Midian. He spent 40 years, a time referred to as "that long period" (Ex. 2:23) in obscurity out of the mainstream of life as he had known it. While the problem he left unsolved in Egypt didn't change, Moses did. God worked in his life, tempering his spirit and molding him into an instrument which He would use in a mighty way.

## Lessons of Obscurity

The *American Heritage Dictionary* defines *obscure* as: "inconspicuous; out of sight; hidden; undistinguished; unknown." Although obscurity is a common experience, we usually try to avoid it or escape from it. We just don't like to be out of circulation.

During the past six months, you may have been out of town, out of the state, or perhaps, out of the country. I can remember one experience, however, in which I found myself "out of the world." It happened in 1970 when I was sent to Southeast Asia.

Vietnam was not considered part of the world by those stationed there. Servicemen were always asking each other, "Where are you from in the world?" Others talked incessantly of the time when they would get back to "the world." Wherever Vietnam was, it was considered nowhere.

The basic objective after arriving was to leave. The one thing every GI wanted out of Vietnam was himself. The first item I was issued when I checked into my unit was my own personal "short-timer's calendar." It was a picture divided into 365 separate parts. Each day I had the privilege of coloring in one more section, until that magic day when the last one was filled and I could board a "freedom bird" for my flight back to the world.

At every Noncommissioned Officers' Club, Officers' Club, or USO facility, the show band invariably closed its performance by playing a chorus of "We gotta get outta this place, if it's the last thing we ever do." Everyone always stood and sang with great enthusiasm.

In Vietnam a common feeling was that life had stopped and couldn't begin again until the war experience was over. There was a strong sense that, "What I had planned for my life has been interrupted and right now there's nothing useful happening. There is no possibility of happiness or significance in this place."

Yet I had one encounter with a man who saw things from a different perspective. One evening at a small worship service, he stood up and explained that though he desperately missed his wife and children, he was convinced that God had put him in Vietnam for a reason. He wanted to learn the lessons God had to teach him while he was there.

That man was a helicopter pilot and flew the Army's most unglamorous aircraft—a flying crane. It was a spindly-legged hunk of steel that was almost all engine. A flying crane was, in effect, an airborne wrecker. It was used to recover battle-damaged and disabled aircraft and equipment and return them to safety for repairs.

That man, flying his airborne scrap metal truck, was learning the lessons of obscurity. I never knew his name or met him again after that night. But the impact of his brief testimony remains with me.

## Growing through the Cutback

Our experiences of being curtailed vary widely. For one person, it may be a physical handicap or a hospital bed. For another, it is perhaps a job loss, a serious moral failure, bankruptcy, or personal loss. A relationship broken through death or dissolution can also produce the feeling that life has stopped and may never begin again.

Though our experiences vary widely, the issue is the same: will we simply *go* through this experience of being cut back—or will we *grow* through it? Our response is the key.

In 1519, Hernando Cortes landed at Veracruz to begin his conquest of Mexico. After unloading about 650 men and their supplies on the beach, Cortes set fire to his fleet of 11 ships. I wonder how those soldiers felt as they watched their only means of transportation back to Spain crackle into charred ruins. With the ocean at their backs and the battle before them, they probably felt closed in.

And Moses, in Midian, must have felt the same way. It seemed that he was in limbo. He had gone from a situation where he held a key position to one where no one even cared if he existed. A most important chapter of his life had ended. A door had closed behind him and Moses felt that he could never go back through it. To him, it had closed permanently.

In addition, the future was unknown. Moses had no idea how long his desert situation would last. There was no fixed point on which he could focus and say, "If only I can hold out until . . . " Time in Midian was a vague question mark. There was no end in sight.

But notice that Moses chose to *live* in Midian. He could have chosen to die there. He could have given up on life altogether and simply quit. But Moses chose to live—and so must we.

It makes little difference whether we find ourselves in Midian through our own mistakes or through circumstances beyond our control. If we have blundered, sinned, failed God and others, then we need to acknowledge this to our heavenly Father, accept His forgiveness by faith, and begin to live where we are. If our curtailment is the result of forces outside ourselves, our choice is between bitterness over what might have been, and the possibilities of what can be.

## Living in Obscurity

New beginnings, whenever and wherever they occur, are God's gracious gifts to us. " 'For I know the plans I have for you,' declares the Lord, 'plans to prosper you and not to harm you, plans to give you hope and a future' " (Jer. 29:11).

The ordinariness of life in Midian must have seemed like a real comedown from Pharaoh's courts in Egypt. Yet God was teaching Moses valuable lessons. Moses was thrust into another culture, another geographical location, and another family. The nomadic life of shepherding introduced him to an existence which would be his life as the leader of God's people. In addition, Moses was being stretched by God, and taught by Him to know more about His presence in daily living. Moses' spark of faith was being slowly kindled into flame.

The decision to live, even though it seems that life has become unlivable, enables us to learn in the ordinariness of each day.

Noted journalist and educator, David Hacker, speaking of the type of student he most wanted in his journalism classes, said: "I want the most alert, inquisitive, excitable minds available and those that have the widest-ranging interests. I want someone who speaks languages, who understands art and music, poetry and dancing and ballet, who knows rifles and shotguns, chemistry and pork production, who has waded in cow manure, who has gone to concerts, and who can be excited by any and all of these things" (James L. Johnson, *Spectrum*, Spring 1980, p. 4).

Mr. Hacker was not speaking of people who had simply been exposed to those things, but who had lived them. People who had endured the hours of disciplined practice to learn music, who had worked long days in a chemistry lab or a packing plant. While most of us would like to do great things for God, few of us enjoy the way He often prepares us in seemingly dead-end situations.

While obscurity fails to capture our imagination and interest, it plays a significant part in the lives of people who have brought about great change. Joseph had his years of servitude and prison (Gen. 39—41); John the Baptist "grew and became strong in spirit and lived in the desert until he appeared publicly to Israel" (Luke 2:80); following his conversion, Paul "went immediately into Arabia," to be alone with God (Gal. 1:17). God often uses situations in which our normal activities are altered to teach us what we either can't or won't learn when things are going smoothly.

In his book *Young Pillars* (Warner Press), which is a caricature of teenagers in the church, cartoonist Charles Schulz depicts a young man telling a girl about all the pins on his sweater: "These are perfect attendance pins . . . Sunday School, Youth Fellowship, Youth Leader Training, Men's Brotherhood, Youth Work Night, Men's Work Night, Youth Missions, Youth Recreation, Vacation School, Bible Camp, Youth Bible Camp, City Youth Camp, County Youth Camp, State Youth

Camp, International Youth Camp, and Choir Practice. . . . I haven't been home in three months!" Before God can deal with us about who we are and who He is, He must often strip away our masks of activity.

It has been said that "Man's extremity is God's opportunity." When Moses arrived in Midian, he had nothing left but God. Everything else was left behind in Egypt. His dreams were shattered, his personal possessions were gone, his former position and prestige were only memories. But like Moses, we often have to reach a point like that before we are ready to be trained and used by God.

## Coping with Obscurity

During our days of curtailment, we must cope with the feeling of living in obscurity. For those of us who dream of making an impact on our world, it is a frustrating feeling to deal with. We keep asking, "How can I make an impact on anything from here—doing this?"

In reality, there is no such thing as obscurity for a child of God. Feelings of obscurity come from within ourselves—when our narrow viewpoints are focused on our own feelings of being unnoticed and neglected. Feelings of obscurity result from a faulty view of ourselves and God.

William Beebe, a naturalist, tells of evenings spent with Teddy Roosevelt at Sagamore Hill. After an evening of talk, the two would walk out on the lawn and search the skies for a certain spot of light beyond the lower left-hand corner of the Great Square of Pegasus. Then Roosevelt would recite: "That is the Spiral Galaxy in Andromeda. It is as large as our Milky Way. It is one of a hundred million galaxies. It consists of one hundred billion suns, each larger than our sun." Then Roosevelt would grin and say, "Now I think we are small enough! Let's go to bed" (*Bits and Pieces,* January 1980).

Little is said in the Scriptures about the need to be recognized. There is, however, a great deal said about the need to be faithful. A number of years ago, a well-known evangelist shared with a small group his firm conviction that the greatest accomplishments of our lives are probably not the "great things" for which we are recognized by others. "Instead," he said, "they are our day-to-day encounters with individuals and our personal, unnoticed outreach to them." Faithfulness doesn't need a stage upon which to act; it simply requires an opportunity.

Perhaps there aren't many famous people buried in Goodland, Kansas, but I know of at least one faithful person who is. His name was Bart. Though he was old enough to be my father, his kindness and sensitivity made him my friend. During the years we worked together on a Colorado ranch, we hunted cattle in snowstorms, loaded hay in the scorching sun, used bailing wire to hold the equipment together, and laughed a lot about our experiences.

At Bart's funeral, a friend and I shared with his widow, Iva, the fact that we represented literally hundreds of people who couldn't be there—scores of people who had worked with us on the ranch; families who had visited the ranch as guests; others who had known Bart before and after his ranch days—all of whom had been helped, challenged, and encouraged by his life.

Bart lived a life of significance in a context of obscurity. He never finished high school, never made a lot of money, never traveled the world. He loved God, loved his wife and family, loved life and other people. From a human perspective, Bart's life may have been ordinary. But the results of his life are eternal because he was faithful.

## Learning in Humility

Let's consider two of the prime lessons which we can learn during days of seeming obscurity. First, *God is sufficient for our needs, wherever we are*. We can see Moses' growth in this area through the naming of his two sons.

His first son was named *Gershom*, which means, "I have become an alien in a foreign land." The name centered on Moses' plight, his problem, and his needs after his escape from Egypt. Even with the spark of faith in his heart, he was definitely "*under* the circumstances."

Moses' second son was named *Eliezer*, "My God is my Helper." Here the focus is on God as the One who is meeting Moses' needs in the midst of hardship and obscurity. This name speaks of growth in faith and of Moses' experience of God's hand on his life.

Nearly two decades ago, a young man faced the crushing news from a Christian organization that he could not represent them as a missionary. The desire of his heart for several years had been to serve Christ in a foreign country through that particular organization. But he was rejected.

In the aftermath of that devastating news, he took a job as a cook at a mountain resort recently purchased by a Christian friend. Just as the summer season started, a fire destroyed the main lodge which contained the kitchen and dining room facilities. The former owner said that the resort was ruined. He predicted that the new owner (the Christian) could not possibly come back from a setback of that magnitude.

But the novice owner and his novice cook believed that Almighty God could and would undergird them. They purchased some used kitchen equipment and moved it into a small building. It was a cook's nightmare—cramped, understaffed, and under-equipped.

The dining room was so small that the staff and the guests were served in shifts—sometimes up to eight separate meals a day. After meals all dishes, pots, and pans were washed by hand with hot water heated on the stove.

Years later, this man served as a missionary in the Middle East with the organization that had originally turned him down. He said of those days at the resort, "I learned that if God could meet my needs and get me through those long days in that little kitchen, He could meet my needs in any situation." That lesson, learned in a tiny kitchen, came during the dark days that followed a crushing disappointment. It is a lesson all of God's change agents must learn at some time, in some place.

A second lesson of obscurity is that *God has called us, first and foremost, to glorify Him;* we can do this in any circumstance of life. We can glorify God in a hospital bed, a rest home, a wheelchair, a home kitchen, a large city, a small town, a prison, a military barracks, a college dormitory—anywhere! Nothing can prevent us from bringing glory to God.

Yet we tend to view our obscure situations to mean that we are no longer useful to God. Often our feelings of uselessness can be traced to our misunderstanding of God's concept of what is useful. In our thinking, *useful* means healthy, mobile, active, outgoing, and happy. God's idea is not so narrow.

We also confuse usefulness with visibility. We value the high visibility gifts of speaking, teaching, entertaining, and leading—gifts that put those who possess them before the eyes of people. But the Apostle Paul likens the church of Jesus Christ to a body in which every member, visible or not, is useful and plays an important part.

> Now the body is not made up of one part but of many. If the foot should say, "Because I am not a hand, I do not belong to the body," it would not for that reason cease to be part of the body. And if the ear should say, "Because I am not an eye, I do not belong to the body," it would not for that reason cease to be part of the body. If the whole body were an eye, where would the sense of hearing be? If the whole body were an ear, where would the sense of smell be? But in fact God has arranged the parts in the body, every one of them, just as He wanted them to be. If they were all one part, where would the body be? As it is, there are many parts, but one body.
>
> The eye cannot say to the hand, "I don't need you!" And the head cannot say to the feet, "I don't need you!" On the contrary, those parts of the body that seem to be weaker are indispensable, and the parts that we think are less honorable we treat with special honor. And the parts that are unpresentable are treated with special modesty, while our presentable parts need no special treatment. But God has combined the members of the body and has given greater honor to the parts that lacked it, so that there should be no division in the body, but that its parts should have equal concern for each other. If one part suffers, every part suffers with it; if one part is honored, every part rejoices with it.
>
> Now you are the body of Christ, and each one of you is a part of it.

1 Cor. 12:14-27

Try a little experiment. When you finish reading this chapter, take your pancreas out, put it in the refrigerator and leave it there for a couple of days. You probably won't miss it, will you? After all, you haven't given your pancreas any thought for months. It's not a highly visible part of the body. We call smart people "brains," we talk about the "big hearts" of generous people, and put a lot of stock in other parts of the body. But what would a friend of yours do if you referred to him as a "pancreas"?

With your pancreas in the refrigerator, your body would be without certain necessary digestive juices and without insulin. The pancreas isn't visible, but it *is* necessary and useful. Without it you would soon die.

Obscurity is where many of us learn that God is sufficient to meet all of our needs, right where we are. It is also a place where we can learn that visibility and usefulness are not the same. Unnoticed and immobile, we can still bring glory to God. While obscurity may prepare some of us for a more visible ministry, for others it may be our life service for God.

It is probable that days of curtailment, in some form, lie in the past, present, and future of each of our lives. Can we thank God for them and accept them from His hand to accomplish His purpose in our lives?

# STUDY QUESTIONS

1. Is there anything about your life today that causes you to feel that you are in a period of curtailment?

2. Have you ever experienced the feeling of being "boxed in," when the door on a chapter of your life has closed and the future remains a blank? What was most helpful to you during that time?

3. What is the most difficult circumstance you face now in your life? What do you think God may want to teach you through it?

4. Since we have been called to "glorify God," what are some specific ways we can do this?

5. In what area of your life can a proper understanding of the difference between "visibility" and "usefulness" help you appreciate your own importance and contribution?

# 6
# Capturing the World's Attention

We who are living in Western society today are suffering from an information overload. Our air waves are filled with sounds and pictures, just waiting to be plucked out and amplified by our receivers. The latest figures show that in more than 33½ million American households, there are two or more television sets. In addition, there are an average of six radio sets per American home. Our automobiles are moving sound systems and communications centers. We can listen to the London Philharmonic on cassette and at the same time, talk to the 18-wheeler in front of us with our CB radio. Our homes are filled with books, newspapers, and magazines that we never seem to finish reading. The amount of information we process each day is staggering.

Review your own life for a few moments. Perhaps you listen to the radio or TV as you dress in the morning. Commercials, public service announcements, words, and music stimulate your memory. By the time you sit down to breakfast, you may be processing appeals urging you to give to the March of Dimes, buy a new car, or join the Pepsi generation. And as Barbra Striesand and Neil Diamond musically lament the fact that "You Don't Bring Me Flowers," you may be reminded of emotions that you'd rather not remember. So you switch off the radio and start reading the back of the cereal box instead. You've been bombarded with messages and you haven't even left for work yet.

Each day brings a new assault on our senses. A multinational company recently sent a direct mail advertisement to executives. Their product was a speed-reading course. Their statistic: The modern American executive must read 1 million words a week just to keep up with the written communications connected with his business. One million words!

## Selective Listening

Faced with this media glut, we have each developed a highly refined state of inattention. On the subconscious level, we simply filter out a large portion of the sensory impressions that come to us each day. Years ago, Alvin Toffler noted in *Future Shock* (Random House) that the average American was hit by a minimum of 560 advertising messages each day. But, of the 560 to which he was exposed, he noticed only 76. In effect, Toffler was saying that in 1970, we blocked out 484 advertising messages a day in order to devote our attention to other things. Since that time, the amount of information and its flow have both increased drastically.

On the conscious level, we use "selectivity." Simply put, this means that we avoid certain messages before we're ever exposed to them. The following story has become almost legendary in the advertising industry, but it illustrates the point.

A number of years ago, when television was just beginning to enjoy its heyday and advertisers were reveling in the belief that millions of people were watching their commercials, distressing news came from an unexpected source. Employees of the water department in a large city noticed that during the prime time viewing hours of 7-10 P.M. there was a marked increase in water consumption on the quarter and half hour. After much consideration, it was decided that the increased water consumption came as TV viewers dashed for the bathroom during the mid- and post-program commercials. In the advertising industry, this became known as the "flush factor." Advertisers faced the awful truth that whenever their message was broadcast, probably a large percentage of people weren't even seeing it.

We are a society of dial twisters and button pushers. Program producers know it. That's why the first few moments of a television program try to capture the viewer's attention. Advertisers know this too. In some cases, the production costs for a 30-second commercial are higher than the costs for a 30-minute program!

As we become more and more selective, we tend to avoid messages we don't agree with. If we're Republicans and a Democratic candidate comes on the radio, we're likely to hit the button rather than listen to an opposing political view. We do it with music we don't like, commercials, radio preachers, personal conversations, children's requests, spouse's criticisms, and a host of other things. The motto of our selectivity syndrome is: "We don't want to hear it."

## The Attention Barrier

For several years, I taught junior high in an aged, two-story building on the west side of Colorado Springs. The windows in my second floor classroom offered an excellent view of the surrounding neighborhood. For that reason, I kept the blinds closed most of the time.

One day as my students were sitting enthralled by my explanation of intransitive verbs, a fire engine screamed to a stop on the street below. One student jumped to his feet, jerked up the blinds, and shouted, "Fire!"

Out the windows, I could see the flames beginning to leap up from an unattached garage half a block away. At that point, I did what any dedicated teacher would have done. I invited the entire class to the window so we could all see what was happening. Intransitive verbs were no match for a fire.

As we watched, the fire raged through the old wooden garage, consuming it in a matter of minutes. About all the fire department could do was cool down the ashes. We watched the radical transformation by fire, then reluctantly went back to intransitive verbs.

For those of us who seek to be agents of spiritual change in a world that pays little heed to God, there is a formidable attention barrier to overcome. The process through which God leads us to capture the attention of the world may be quite different from the one we expect Him to use:

> There the angel of the Lord appeared to him in flames of fire
> from within a bush. Moses saw that though the bush was on fire
> it did not burn up. So Moses thought, *I will go over and see this
> strange sight—why the bush does not burn up* (Ex. 3:2-3).

Moses was not drawn to the burning bush simply because it was on fire. He was intrigued because it burned, but was not consumed. Usually, a fire consumes material during the process of burning. We don't expect something which has been burned to look the same as it did before the fire. Moses was attracted by a supernatural event—a bush that was on fire, but was not burned up.

## Capturing Attention

Some years ago my wife and I lived and worked on a guest ranch in the Colorado mountains. A Christian couple we knew came to spend a few days there following the death of their 8-year-old son. Their boy had fought an agonizing battle against leukemia for 18 months. After his funeral, they came to the mountains for a few days just to rest, be together, and spend much time in fellowship with God.

At breakfast one morning, they were seated with another guest, the headmistress of a prestigious, private school. As they visited, the conversation turned to family and children. Without eavesdropping, I was aware that the focus of their conversation was on the death of this couple's son and how their personal relationship with Christ had enabled them to face it. They talked for almost two hours.

As they passed the office on their way out of the dining room, the headmistress gripped my friend's arm and said: "I want to know why you don't hate God for what He did to your son. I don't know of anyone who could go through what you did and not be overwhelmed with bitterness and anger."

You see, she had seen a Christian going through the fire, but not being consumed. It was a supernatural event and it got her attention. If people in the world wanted to hear a sermon, they would be in church. Your friends without Christ probably won't be interested in this book, and they won't care about most Christian films and TV programs. But when they see someone whose life is engulfed by the flames of adversity, but who is not being consumed, they will take notice.

To capture the inattentive hearts and minds of those without Jesus Christ, I believe that God employs the same technique He used with Moses. The modern world pauses and pays attention when it sees a Christian who is "in the fire, but not consumed."

The Apostle Peter urged us: "But in your hearts, set apart Christ as Lord. Always be prepared to give an answer to everyone who asks you to give the reason for the hope that you have" (1 Peter 3:15). Has anyone ever asked you to tell him the reason for the hope that you have?

In our efforts to guard against projecting Christianity as dull and drab, we often wrongly assume that a Christian's attractiveness should come from a happy smile and an airy demeanor that lets others know that life is fantastic. But hope shines brightest against the dark background of despair.

## The Survivors

Perhaps Christianity's greatest impact on those who ignore God comes from the person who experiences events that should disintegrate his life—yet with the presence of the Saviour, he is not devastated by them. Peter went on to write:

> Dear friends, do not be surprised at the painful [fiery] trial you are suffering, as though something strange were happening to you. But rejoice that you participate in the sufferings of Christ, so that you may be overjoyed when His glory is revealed (1 Peter 4:12-13).

We naturally think that we are most effective as agents of change when we can influence others from a position of strength and success. But we need God's divine perspective to correct our faulty human view. A glance at the life of one of the first century's greatest change agents, the Apostle Paul, should help.

After Paul met Christ, he started preaching. As a result, the Jews conspired to kill him. As we pick up the narrative in Acts 9:23, we see Paul leaving the city of Damascus under the cover of darkness. When he reached Jerusalem, he tried to join the disciples. But they were all afraid of him. They knew he had been persecuting Christians and wouldn't touch him with a seven-cubit pole.

Paul's later travels were anything but a trail of successes. At Paphos, he encountered opposition. In Iconium, there was a plot to stone him and he fled the city. At Lystra, the plot succeeded. He was stoned and left for dead. In Philippi, Paul was thrown in jail, stripped, and beaten. In

Thessalonica, there was a riot. Paul took another "night coach flight" out of the city.

Moses was hardly at the zenith of success when he approached the burning bush. His resumé was a little shaky there on the far side of the desert. After 40 years, he was still taking care of his father-in-law's sheep. No flock of his own? No initiative? No ambition? Yet this is precisely the point at which God called Moses to do great things for Him.

We would all like to be change agents who arrive clothed in the fashionable trappings of success. But we are not disqualified if we happen to show up in garments of affliction. In the bright light of Scripture, it would seem that adverse circumstances often provide us with greater opportunities to function as agents of change than do our successes.

My experience during the past years with a group of single adults has convinced me that the burning bush which isn't consumed is still being used by God as an attention-getter. These single people, through the aftershock of divorce, child custody disputes, the death of a spouse, unfulfilled longings for marriage, and other painful trials, have shown the reality of Christ's power to people around them.

Often their testimony has been one, not of overwhelming victory at the moment, but of survival. They have cast their burdens on the Lord and found that He sustains them. And their friends and families have noticed. Far from a pinnacle of achievement, they have testified of their faith in the furnace of affliction, but they have been heard. They have broken through the barrier of inattention and God is using them to effect changes in the lives of others, many of whom haven't given a thought to God in years.

As God's agents of change, we must learn that our sovereign Lord both ordains and allows the circumstances with which we function for Him in this world. We must learn to draw our strength from Him and to make the most of whatever situation we find ourselves in. And we must realize that our greatest opportunities to bring change may come while we think we are on the bottom of the heap. "Under the circumstances." In the pits.

Paul had a problem with a thorn in the flesh. Whatever it was, he experienced it as a tremendous source of torment. He pleaded with God to remove it and received this answer:

But He said to me, "My grace is sufficient for you, for My power is made perfect in weakness." Therefore I will boast all the more gladly about my weaknesses, so that Christ's power may rest on me. That is why, for Christ's sake, I delight in weaknesses, in insults, in hardships, in persecutions, in difficulties. For when I am weak, then I am strong (2 Cor. 12:9-10).

God captured Moses' attention with a bush that burned, but was not consumed. He may choose to use us, as His agents of change, in the same way in the lives of our friends, associates, and even our enemies.

I will go over and see this strange sight—why the bush does not burn up (Ex. 3:3).

# STUDY QUESTIONS

1. How would you describe the "flush factor" that exists in our efforts to communicate the Gospel of Christ to our friends and associates?

2. Look up these New Testament passages on suffering and examine them in light of the idea of capturing the world's attention (2 Cor. 1:3-11; 1 Peter 3:13-17; 2 Peter 4:12-19; Phil. 3:7-10).

3. What should you do if you are suffering and no one seems to be paying attention?

4. What got your attention when you first seriously considered becoming a Christian?

5. As a Christian agent of change, how do you find the concept of "selective attention" at work in your own life?

# 7
# Called

After God got Moses' attention at the burning bush, they had a remarkable conversation. In it, one of the most capable, highly trained men on earth at that time threw every excuse in the world at a holy God from whom he had just hid in fear. This glimpse of Moses strikes me as moving, humorous, absurd, and genuinely human—all at the same time.

## God Calls Moses

Without attempting to add to the words of divine inspiration, I have tried to place myself next to Moses' sandals as God spoke to him. I've wondered if Moses' thoughts might have been something like this (see Ex. 3:7-10):

The Lord said: "I HAVE INDEED SEEN THE MISERY OF MY PEOPLE IN EGYPT."

> "Man, am I glad. They're really bad off. Somebody needs to do something about that situation. I was beginning to wonder if there even was a God who cared. But He is aware of the problem. Great!"

"I HAVE HEARD THEM CRYING OUT BECAUSE OF THEIR SLAVE DRIVERS, AND I AM CONCERNED ABOUT THEIR SUFFERING."

"Now we're getting down to the issue. Oppression! I tried to do something about that 40 years ago. Now God knows and is getting involved. He's concerned. He has compassion. Praise the Lord, He understands their suffering."

"SO I HAVE COME DOWN TO RESCUE THEM FROM THE HAND OF THE EGYPTIANS."

"Beautiful! God is going to act. He has come down to rescue them. Fantastic! The long period of waiting is over. Hang on for a miracle!"

". . . AND TO BRING THEM UP OUT OF THAT LAND INTO A GOOD AND SPACIOUS LAND, A LAND FLOWING WITH MILK AND HONEY—THE HOME OF THE CANAANITES, HITTITES, AMORITES, PERIZZITES, HIVITES, AND JEBUSITES."

"All right! Not only is God going to get them out of Egypt, He's going to give them a country of their own. The Canaanites, Hittites, and all the other *ites* will just have to lump it. This is too good to be true! Keep going, Lord."

"AND NOW THE CRY OF THE ISRAELITES HAS REACHED ME, AND I HAVE SEEN THE WAY THE EGYPTIANS ARE OPPRESSING THEM."

"Yes! Preach it, Lord! You have heard their cry, seen their oppression. You are going to move into action!"

"SO NOW, GO."

"Yes! Go, Lord. Go get'em. Give it to Pharaoh. Deliver Your people. Show Your power. Head'em up, move'em out!"

"I AM SENDING *YOU* TO PHARAOH TO BRING MY PEOPLE, THE ISRAELITES, OUT OF EGYPT."

"I . . . uh . . . would You run that part by me one more time?"

Moses was ready for God to move in and make the change. The

problem was that Moses saw this as a strategic maneuver, sort of a divine B-52 mission. He wanted the Lord to bomb Egypt into submission and let the Israelites out of their prison camp and into freedom. But Moses wasn't expecting to be named general in charge of a ground operation.

A passage from Paul's letter to the Ephesians helps us see the proper relationship of God's part to our part in the process of change.

**Now to Him who is able to do immeasurably more than all we ask or imagine . . .**

That's the first part. That's where Moses was as he knelt by the burning bush. "Go get'em, Lord!" But the verse continues:

**. . . according to His power that is at work within us.**

God does give us opportunities to participate in strategic changes at a distance through intercessory prayer. But He also calls us to be personally involved with others as His power works *in* and *through* our lives. The passage concludes:

**. . . to Him be glory in the church and in Christ Jesus throughout all generations, forever and ever! Amen** (Eph. 3:20-21).

God's work through our lives is designed to bring glory to Him through the person of Jesus Christ. As agents of spiritual change, God's glory must be our ultimate aim and the ultimate test of our motives and methods.

## Who Are You?

But Moses said to God, "Who am I, that I should go to Pharaoh and bring the Israelites out of Egypt?" (Ex. 3:11)

*Who am I?* Forty years before, as a prince in Egypt, Moses would have never asked that question. But in his own estimation, he had dropped quite a few points on the scale and was staggered by the prospect of returning to Egypt.

*Who am I?* It's a question many people are still asking. We live in an age when self-discovery has become a religion of its own. The inscription at the ancient Delphic oracle said, "Know thyself." Today we can walk into any bookstore and find several best-sellers that will tell us how to know ourselves. Popular magazines are filled with articles on self-analysis and fulfillment. Author Tom Wolfe dubbed the 1970s as "The Me Generation"—the generation that spawned a new magazine titled simply, *Self*.

*Who am I?* For Moses and for us, it is a significant question. But when it comes to God's call in our lives, it is also *the wrong question*. It is a question that God did not answer for Moses. Instead, He gave Moses the answer to the question he should have asked. God's answer was, "I will be with you."

Moses' next question moved closer to the real issue as he asked how he should identify the God who had sent him. "God said to Moses, 'I am who I am. This is what you are to say to the Israelites: 'I AM has sent me to you' " (Ex. 3:14).

The question for God's change agent is not *Who am I?* but rather *Who are You?* The answer to the first question can leave us with either an inflated sense of our own importance or writhing in the throes of despair over our inadequacy. We are seldom able to answer the question of our identity in a balanced, objective sense. But as we ask *Who are You?* we encounter the One who says, "I will be with you." God's change agents are called, not on the basis of who they are, but on the basis of who God is.

## Our Multidimensional God

In the pages of Scripture we discover the multidimensional God who has called us into His service. In Old and New Testaments alike, we see His unique blend of awesome power and gentle love.

> The Lord builds up Jerusalem; He gathers the exiles of Israel. He heals the broken-hearted and binds up their wounds. He determines the number of the stars and calls them each by name. Great is our Lord and mighty in power; His understanding has no limit. The Lord sustains the humble but casts the wicked to the ground (Ps. 147:2-6).
>
> Yours, O Lord, is the greatness and the power and the glory and the majesty and the splendor, for everything in heaven and

earth is Yours. Yours, O Lord, is the kingdom; You are exalted as Head over all. Wealth and honor come from You; You are the Ruler of all things. In Your hands are strength and power to exalt and give strength to all. Now, our God, we give You thanks and praise Your glorious name (1 Chron. 29:11-13).

To Him who is able to keep you from falling and to present you before His glorious presence without fault, and with great joy—to the only God our Saviour be glory, majesty, power, and authority, through Jesus Christ our Lord, before all ages, now and forevermore! Amen (Jude 24-25).

This is the God whom we are to know in a deeper way each day. And to do that takes time. There are no spiritual TV dinners available to nourish our hunger for the Almighty. Microwave spirituality is nonexistent. Hurried prayers and speed-reading the Bible will not adequately acquaint us with God.

In his classic book, *Your God Is Too Small*, British theologian J.B. Phillips says:

We shall never want to serve God in our real and secret hearts if He looms in our subconscious mind as an arbitrary Dictator or a Spoilsport, or as one who takes advantage of His position to make us poor mortals feel guilty and afraid. We have not only to be impressed by the ''size'' and unlimited power of God; we have to be moved to genuine admiration, respect, and affection, if we are ever to worship Him (MacMillan, p. 63).

William Archibald Spooner was a 19th century Englishman who frequently got his words mixed up. In fact, Spooner did it so often that a slip of the tongue became known as a ''spoonerism.'' Spooner became known for such immortal phrases as ''blushing crow'' instead of ''crushing blow,'' and a ''half-warmed fish'' instead of ''half-formed wish.''

When a friend of mine first began memorizing Bible verses, someone noticed his small pack of Scripture cards and asked what he was doing. He meant to reply, ''I'm reviewing a verse,'' but what came out was, ''I'm reversing a view.''

I think his slip was closer to the truth. Paul challenged the Christians at Rome, "Don't let the world around you squeeze you into its own mold, but let God remold your minds from within" (Rom. 12:2, PH). As we study the Bible, memorize it, meditate on it, and use its words of praise in prayer, God reverses our faulty human views about who He is.

God has called us on the basis of who He is *and* on the basis of His promise to be with us. Paul wrote to the Ephesians:

> I keep asking that the God of our Lord Jesus Christ, the glorious Father, may give you the Spirit of wisdom and revelation, so that you may know Him better. I pray also that the eyes of your heart may be enlightened in order that you may know the hope to which He has called you, the riches of His glorious inheritance in the saints, and His incomparably great power for us who believe (Eph. 1:17-19).

The arena of change in which we fight is filled with impossible situations. We are called to forgive in the face of great wrong done; reconcile relationships that seem irrevocably severed; continue to love even after hatred is returned; stand before a tidal wave of evil and seek to send it reeling backward by simply doing good.

Our encouragement is that the God who has called us stands with us in every situation. Christ is not an absentee landlord. He does not send us into a slum and offer written suggestions from afar for maintenance and repair. Rather, He indwells us and equips us for the work to which He calls us.

## Cooperation in Change

"Cooperation in change" describes our relationship with God and His work in the world. He has given us the privilege of working alongside Him for change.

After 40 years of preparation in the wilderness of Midian, Moses was far from perfect—and he knew it. In spite of all the lessons learned and the nurturing of the spark of faith in his life, he was still reluctant to try again where he had failed years before. Later in Moses' conversation with God, the Lord asked:

"WHAT IS THAT IN YOUR HAND?"

If I had been in Moses' place, my thoughts might well have run in the following vein:

> "What do I have in my hand? A staff. It could have been a scepter if I hadn't blown it. It was a dumb thing to do, killing that Egyptian. If I'd kept my cool, I might have eventually risen to a high place in the government, maybe even become Pharaoh, and then I could have set my entire nation free. But I don't have a scepter in my hand right now.
>
> "It's just a staff, Lord. For the past 40 years, I haven't wanted anything else. Leadership just isn't my thing. You can look at my record and figure that out. No, this staff is the symbol of everything I should be, but am not. It's the reminder of something I wanted more than anything else in the world, and I ruined it."

The Lord said: "THROW IT ON THE GROUND."

> "Throw it down? I know it's only a staff, Lord, but it's all I've got. Right now, it's me, my identity, my job, my life. Throw it down? And have nothing to hang onto? This is crazy, absurd. Take the only thing I have left and throw it down? I don't understand, but if You say so. . . ."

"Moses threw it on the ground and it became a snake, and he ran from it" (Ex. 4:3). When God takes what we have, as we offer it to Him, and begins to work with it, the results can be frightening—as Moses discovered.

Then the Lord said to him: "REACH OUT YOUR HAND AND TAKE IT BY THE TAIL."

So Moses picked it up and it turned back into a staff. Isn't it interesting that it didn't turn into a scepter? God didn't restore Moses to a position of authority in Egypt. His past choices weren't negated by God's calling him right where he was, as he was. But when Moses left for Egypt in obedience to God's call and command, "he took the staff of God in his hand" (Ex. 4:20). That is what each of us, as God's change agents, desperately needs. And that is what God will give us as we take what we have in our hands and offer it to Him.

What do you have in your hand today? A calculator, a vacuum cleaner, a piece of chalk, a steering wheel, a brick and trowel, a wet diaper, a wad of money, a stethoscope, a pen, a hammer? Whatever it is, lay it down. Present it to God as an offering to be used by Him in whatever way He chooses.

## The Right Perspective

There is a beautiful parallel in the New Testament that reminds us that whatever we have is enough when we give it to God. When Jesus and His disciples were confronted by a crowd of 5,000 hungry people, Jesus asked Philip, "Where shall we buy bread for these people to eat?" Philip's response might be accurately paraphrased as: "There is no place to buy, no money to buy with—no way to feed them." (See John 6:7.)

From Philip's perspective, Jesus and the disciples were totally out of luck in the resources department. They couldn't pull it off even if McDonald's were right around the corner and they had a 200 denarii gift certificate.

Andrew, on the other hand, had noticed that a boy had five small barley loaves and two small fish, roughly the equivalent of five crackers and two sardines. Hardly enough to feed 5,000 people. While Philip saw it as a total impossibility, with no resources available, Andrew saw it as a situation in which they had a little bit, but such a little bit that it was hardly worth thinking about. He said, "How far will they go among so many?"

When God calls us into cooperation with Him in His work of change, we often view ourselves as the disciples did. "No way. I haven't got anything that's needed to do this work."

Or as Andrew reasoned, "I've got a little bit of what it takes, but it's so little and the need is so great."

What we have *is* too little until, like the disciple, we bring it to Jesus and He blesses it. You see, like Moses, God asks us what we have in our hands. Then He asks us to give it to Him. And then, He returns it, empowered by Him to do the job at hand. Whatever we have is enough when we give it to Him.

We are called to be God's agents of change on the basis of who He is, and on the basis of His promise to be with us.

# STUDY QUESTIONS

1. Have you ever been convinced that God wants you to do something, but you are afraid to do it?

2. When you argue with God, on what do you base your argument?

3. List four or five things you feel Moses may have been afraid of as he contemplated returning to Egypt.

4. Why doesn't God just do what He wants to in the world and leave us out of it? Why does He seek human agents of change? How do the following verses show that God works through people to bring about change?

    Ezekiel 22:30

    2 Corinthians 5:18-20

    Ephesians 3:20-21

    Exodus 3:10; 6:13; 14:16

    Isaiah 6:8

5. What do you have in your hand? What does it mean to "lay it down" before God?

# 8
# Constituency

The Israelites were a people who had been ruthlessly used. At one point in their history, Pharaoh had sought to curtail their population growth by forcing them to throw their newborn sons into the river. They were a people whose lives had been made bitter by injustice and hard labor.

Yet their history and tradition told them that this was not what God had planned for them. They knew that what they were experiencing was humanly intolerable. It was a situation which was contrary to God's promises to their great patriarch, Abraham. And in their suffering, they cried out to God.

## What Will People Think?
Moses had failed once with these people. Forty years earlier, a Hebrew had scorned Moses' abortive attempt to help his people by saying: "Who made you a ruler and a judge over us?" Who do you think you are? (see Ex. 2:14)

Moses had been rejected by his own people and exiled into obscurity in the land of Midian. Now he had to face the elders of Israel, and he was scared.

The obstinacy of people can be annoying, frustrating, and also frightening. The late R. G. LeTourneau, developer of giant earthmoving equipment, was called a "mover of men and mountains." Most of us would admit that sometimes mountains seem much easier to move than people. Dealing with people can be unnerving.

Our constituency is the group of people to whom we are responsible. It may be our family, our Sunday School class, our employees, our clients, our customers, our patients, or our students. We may even function as agents of change among many constituencies at the same time. But try to focus on one that is particularly important to you right now.

Why was Moses afraid? The Scriptures give us some direct clues by the questions he asked God at the burning bush:

> Moses said to God, "Suppose I go to the Israelites and say to them, 'The God of your fathers has sent me to you,' and they ask me, 'What is His name?' Then what shall I tell them?" . . . "What if they do not believe me or listen to me and say, 'The Lord did not appear to you'?" (Ex. 3:13; 4:1)

Moses was full of apprehension. How would the elders of Israel respond to his reappearance, since he claimed to be an agent of change sent by God? "What if they ask Your name? What if they don't believe me? What if they question Your appearing to me?" Moses' fear, in large part, was based on assumptions he made about the people he had been called to deliver.

What were some of his assumptions?

He assumed that his first opposition would come from the people who were supposed to be on his side. While "group inertia" does resist change, it is dangerous to assume, before the fact, that your constituency will oppose your efforts at change.

Moses assumed that the elders of Israel would question his authority to lead them. From the evidence of Scripture, we notice that the elders' first reaction was to believe (Ex. 29—31). Questioning did come, but not at the outset as Moses assumed it would.

I believe that Moses assumed that Israel would reject him as they had before. Past experience plays a great role in producing our assumptions. We need to learn from experience. But there is danger—especially if we allow our past to cast shadows on our expectations of today, particularly when we are experiencing God's hand on our lives in a new way.

Other factors can produce apprehension too. One of these factors is *control.* In some cases, your constituency may have the power to hire and fire you. The knowledge that your program of change could cost you your job can be intimidating.

For several years, I taught public school in a district that went through two superintendents in three years. They have recently hired a new man. But the school board's quick dismissal of top personnel has to weigh on this man's mind as he contemplates his future. When your constituency has control of your pocketbook, your occupational status, or both, it's easy to be afraid of moving too fast or in the wrong direction as a change agent.

Fear of our constituency can result from assumptions, control, and *evaluation.* Our apprehension can be the product of nothing more than concern over what people will think of us. Lest we underestimate the power of public opinion in our private lives and in our life as a nation, we need only consider the importance placed on Gallup polls and similar measures of national attitude.

When I began teaching a Sunday morning class of single adults, most of whom were divorced persons in their 30s and 40s, I was plagued by a recurring dream. During my dream, I would be teaching the class. As the lesson progressed, people would get up and leave, many of them shaking their heads and muttering under their breath. This dream began to affect my preparation and my consideration of things which I felt I should say. I found myself increasingly afraid to express them.

After a couple of years of teaching the class and, fortunately, finding my dream unfulfilled, I shared it with my pastor. He said, "You know, I've been plagued myself with the same dream."

Relieved, I said, "You mean about people leaving the church while you're preaching?"

"No," he said, "about people leaving your class while you're teaching!"

Assumptions, control, and evaluation are factors in every situation where we desire to function as agents of change. We all have assumptions about our constituencies. Those assumptions may be positive, negative, right, or wrong, but they are there and we must be aware of their existence. Even if we function in a management or leadership role, those we serve may control significant aspects of our lives. And all of us are affected by the opinions of those we serve.

These points cause tension for agents of spiritual change. We are called to something more than an exercise of raw authoritarian power in our efforts at turning things around. While we may be involved in working for social changes in our world, we should also be constantly aware of people's attitudes toward God and their relationships with Him through faith in Jesus Christ.

From the life of Moses, we can discover five valuable principles to guide us in dealing with the people in whom and through whom we desire to see God work changes.

## Know Your People

Did Moses really know the Israelites? Wasn't he an Israelite himself by birth? Hadn't he spent 40 years living in close proximity with them? His actions and inaccurate assumptions cause us to wonder.

Stephen testified that in Moses' first attempt at turning things around in Egypt, "Moses thought that his own people would realize that God was using him to rescue them, but they did not" (Acts 7:25). Before Moses returned, he gave evidence of several assumptions about the elders of Israel which proved to be false.

When God sent Moses back to Egypt, He placed him right in the middle of the folks he had been called to deliver. We don't know how long it took from Moses' first appearance before Pharaoh, until the Israelites crossed the Red Sea. But this was a time of intensive education for Moses. A change agent doesn't work well when he is physically or psychologically distant from his people.

Bob Mitchell, president of Young Life, tells a story about the importance of getting to know one's people. During a week long summer camp in Colorado, Mitch noticed one young high school boy who seemed remote and uninterested in what was going on. Mitch decided to take on the lad as a personal project. During the week Mitch had the privilege of leading the boy to faith in Jesus Christ. At week's end, he asked the boy when he had first become interested in being a Christian.

The boy replied, "The day you learned my name."

Knowing our people goes far beyond a mere acquaintance or a working knowledge of how to get them to do what we want them to do. It involves getting inside them, thinking, feeling, crying, and rejoicing with them. We must know them, not to accomplish our program, but in order to meet their deep needs.

How do we get to know our people?

- Spend time with them—formal working time and informal social and recreational activities.
- Listen to them.
- Pray for them. Insight often comes during the times when we give ourselves to prayer for them.
- Pray with them.

# Honesty—Present Issues Openly and Accurately

"Moses and Aaron brought together all the elders of the Israelites, and Aaron told them everything the Lord had said to Moses. He also performed the signs before the people, and they believed. And when they heard that the Lord was concerned about them and had seen their misery, they bowed down and worshiped" (Ex. 4:29).

God had instructed Moses to assemble the elders of Israel, and then to tell them that God had appeared to him and had promised to deliver them. Moses obeyed. How simple it seems but how easily we lose sight of the importance of open and accurate communication!

Have you ever tried to soften the impact of the truth by blending in a little "harmless deception"? When you assume that the truth will not accomplish your goals in a particular situation, perhaps your goals need closer examination.

Not long ago, a friend was faced with the unpleasant task of firing an employee. His concern was that this news would cause his employee to slip into the depths of serious depression because of similar previous failures. What should he do?

As my friend, another Christian brother, and I discussed the issue and the options, we sought a scriptural principle to apply. We were reminded of Paul's command that we should be "speaking the truth in love" (Eph. 4:15). The New Testament stresses this principle again and again. As Christians, our dealings with others should be characterized by truthfulness and love. This concept provided a new dimension to the problem.

My friend simply confronted his employee with the bad news. In the past, he had tried many times to help this employee. My friend, in love, shared some thoughts about this man's past performance and made suggestions for the future. Not only was he in a position to do that, but he also had a responsibility as a brother in Christ to do it. In truthfulness, he fired him. In love, he gave him some options and help for the future.

The one thing we are unable to deal with is deception. Deception is a ghost which haunts but eludes any efforts to grasp or dispel it. Deception will wreck a marriage, a business, a church, or a friendship because the parties involved cannot deal with the issues which are at stake. "Better is open rebuke than hidden love. The kisses of an enemy may be profuse, but faithful are the wounds of a friend" (Prov. 27:5-6). Paul wrote, "Do not lie to each other, since you have taken off your old self with its practices" (Col. 3:9).

Truth, on the other hand, may be painful, but it can be met head-on and dealt with. Jesus characterized Himself as "the Way, the Truth, and the Life" (John 14:6). If He indwells us, then we should express His nature of truth to others.

Truth is the medium and message of communication for all who want to work with God to change this world. Truth demands that we function on the basis of principle, rather than expediency. Sometimes, speaking the truth may appear to undermine the whole work in which we are involved. Then we must choose to act on God's principles and trust the outcome to Him, rather than to move ahead with what "looks good."

Presenting issues openly and accurately also requires that we do our homework. Unfortunately, much of our efforts as Christians in this area have been misdirected, resulting from shoddy scholarship and preparation. We have been victimized by our own management technique of "putting out brushfires" instead of focusing on well-thought-out goals and objectives.

For the past several years, the Federal Communications Commission has been trying to stem the tide of letters pouring in from all over the United States, protesting a nonexistent petition allegedly filed by athiest Madalyn Murray O'Hair. The imaginary petition grew out of a request filed by two California men which would have limited the number of radio frequencies available for educational and religious broadcasters. The FCC denied that request. But, within the world of concerned Christians, word began circulating that Mrs. O'Hair had filed a petition which would completely ban religious broadcasting from the nation's airwaves.

The whole process was similar to the parlor game in which one person whispers a phrase to someone who in turn whispers it to another. By the time it makes the rounds of everyone in the room, it isn't even close to the original phrase. At last report, the FCC had hired a public relations firm to answer the mail and disseminate the word that all the reaction had been to an imaginary petition.

## Let God Confirm Your Authority to Lead

I am intrigued by the fact that the first signs given to Moses—the staff which became a snake and the leprous hand—were given to convince the elders of Israel that God had really sent Moses. That sounds like the dream of every change agent who seeks to convince his constituency that he has been divinely appointed for a task. Why doesn't God do that for all of us?

Throughout Moses' dealings with the nation of Israel, God gave some spectacular confirmations of Moses' calling and authority. On one occasion, the earth opened up and swallowed those who opposed Moses (Num. 16:31-32). I always thought that would be a great technique for a junior high teacher to have. Just imagine an unruly student crowd at an all-school assembly refusing to respond to your repeated calls for quiet. All of a sudden the gym floor cracks open and swallows the entire eighth grade. Not a bad move to enhance your authority.

But in my study of Moses' life, I have yet to find an instance when Moses told God how to confirm his (Moses') position and calling. He wisely left that work in God's hands. To do otherwise was to invite disaster and failure.

"Be sure you're right, and then go ahead." That saying has been popularly attributed to Davy Crockett, king of the wild frontier. It would be nice if we could approach our roles as spiritual agents of change in that way, but sometimes we do make mistakes. If God has indeed called us to move in a certain area to bring about change, He will no doubt eventually make that clear to our constituency. Significant, lasting changes take place only when our people give us cooperation and mutual effort. Changes cannot be forced on people.

When the people complained to and challenged Moses, he prayed earnestly, humbly to God. Today, prayer is not a popular solution. Praying about our helplessness, our needs, and our feelings for those who oppose us is not a quick way to cope with a situation. But it is consistent with the teachings of Scripture.

Jesus said that we should "pray for those who persecute" us (Matt. 5:44). Praying for our constituency keeps us from having an adversary relationship with them. Prayer should not be used to call down fire from heaven on our enemies. Rather, it should be used to seek God's work in their lives and in our own.

Paul urged the Christians at Philippi:

Do nothing out of selfish ambition or vain conceit, but in humility consider others better than yourselves. Each of you should look not only to your own interests, but also to the interests of others. Your attitude should be the same as that of Christ Jesus (Phil. 2:3-5).

Through prayer we simply cast ourselves, our calling, and our constituency on God for His mercy and His direction for the future. If there is any confirming to be done, we acknowledge to God that He will have to do it.

Naturally, we want some spectacular signs, like the ones given to Moses, to confirm our authority as God's agents of change. But we must remember that *God confirms the calling of His agents of change*. The signs in Moses' case were merely God's specific method of confirmation which may vary widely.

God may choose to confirm our calling in the eyes of others with signs that are much less spectacular, but no less miraculous. Jesus said, "All men will know that you are My disciples if you love one another" (John 13:35). What is more miraculous than a selfless display of devotion? "The fruit of the Spirit is love, joy, peace, patience, kindness, goodness, faithfulness, gentleness, and self-control. Against such things there is no law" (Gal. 5:22-23).

Not spectacular, but miraculous. Not flashy, but effective—a true confirmation that God lives within us.

## Serve Them in Love and Loyalty

The passage in Philippians 2 goes on to describe how the preexistent Son of God left heaven's glory to become a human member of this fallen creation, and to move through it as a servant. Jesus, the greatest Change Agent of all time, was a true Servant.

Moses served the Israelites as their leader. He tried to change their outlook on life and their understanding of God. In love, Moses served them in the mundane areas of life. He listened to the people's complaints and petitioned God for their daily needs. He wore himself out trying to handle their petty disputes and arguments.

Paul explained his own ministry to the Corinthians by saying, "We do not preach ourselves, but Jesus Christ as Lord, and ourselves as your servants for Jesus' sake" (2 Cor. 4:5). Yet, we have a hard time believing that a leadership role is really one of servanthood. We like it when others tend to *our* needs, not vice versa.

Try to recall a group's most common complaints about someone who was trying to be a change agent. Some examples might be: (1) "He tried to move too fast. We just weren't ready to make changes that big, that soon." (2) "He tried to cram his program down our throats. He only knew what *he* wanted, not what we felt we needed." (3) "She talked a lot to us but seldom took time to listen to how we felt about things." (4) "He kept talking about tightening the organizational belt while he was getting rich." (5) "She cared about where she was going, not about where we were going."

Have you ever heard a group complain about a change agent who served them in love? You probably have. People complained about Jesus, Moses, and Paul. But the principle of serving others in love remains the same even if complaints result from it. The obvious fact is that we will never enjoy a perfect relationship with our constituency. But by serving them in love, we will maximize our efforts at leading them into change and we will maintain a devotion to scriptural principles in both our goals and our methods. We are to wholeheartedly serve them in love, as a service to Christ.

Moses was not just moving through this organization on his way to greater things. He saw himself as having no future besides what God was doing in and through the nation of Israel. At one point, after years of wilderness wandering, God responded to the unbelief and complaints of the people by telling Moses:

> I will strike them down with a plague and destroy them, but I will make you into a nation greater and stronger than they (Num. 14:12).

Most of us would have found it hard to pass up an offer like that. After all, who wouldn't have been sick and tired of those people with their continuing history of rebellion, unbelief, and complaints? Yet Moses reminded God of His promises to bring them up out of Egypt into a Promised Land. He told God that if He destroyed this nation all at once, the Egyptians would hear about it and would ridicule the ability of God to finish what He started. Moses appealed to God's love and forgiveness—all for a people who had given him years of grief and had tried every means possible to undermine his authority and get rid of him.

## Live with a Deep Sense of God's Call

I believe loyalty grows out of a deep sense of God's call. That sense may be sadly lacking many times as we consider and accept positions that place us within groups or organizations as agents of change. Perhaps it is only natural, but for years I have been intrigued by the phenomenon of ministers being "called" to new positions. I have wondered why so few people get called to smaller churches and lower-paying positions than they had before. Why does the movement of ministers of the Gospel look so much like the corporate ladder that claims no official link with the living God?

My questions were brought into sharp focus a couple of years ago when one of the ministers of our church resigned to accept a new position which he believed God had "called" him to. His testimony challenged me to a new awareness of what it means to consider and heed God's call.

As he shared the background of his decision with us, Jim recalled the day a letter from a small, Christian college in North Dakota had arrived. The administrators had offered him a position on their faculty. He and his wife had visited the campus, more out of curiosity than anything else, and had been depressed by the desolate landscape and its location in the "super boonies."

Jim related his silent prayer to God that night after touring the campus: "Lord, after seeing this situation and walking around the campus, I'm just convinced that it's not Your will for us to come here. But just in case there is the remotest possibility that it might be Your will, I just want to let You know that I won't come." He said later that he should have known better than to pray something like that, but that's how he felt.

God began to speak to Jim and make it plain to him that He was calling him to work there. Jim wrestled with leaving the beauty of his hometown, his family, and his well-paid position in a big church for a significantly smaller salary in a smaller town far away. But he decided to go. And by deciding to follow God's leading, Jim helped me understand the deep joy and sense of anticipation that comes when we act on faith, even when it looks like we're going down, instead of up.

Perhaps our ability to effect change is directly related to our commitment to the people we lead and serve. And that commitment seems to be tied in with our deep sense that it is God, not just a nice salary, a nice location, or a step up the ladder, who has caused us to become involved with our particular constituency as an agent of change.

Moses moved from a fear of his constituency to a loyal devotion to them undergirded by the same God who had called and confirmed him as His man in their midst.

# STUDY QUESTIONS

1. Who would you say is your constituency right now in your role as a Christian agent of change?

2. What assumptions have you made about the person(s) with whom you are working toward change?

3. Which one of the following factors—assumptions, control, or evaluation—has the biggest influence on how you feel about your constituency? Does this help or hinder your work with them?

4. What would be your thoughts and struggles if you believed God was calling you to take a step down in salary and status?

5. What evidences of loyalty do you see in Moses' relationship with Israel? Are the same evidences present in your service to your constituency? How can a person maintain a loyal spirit and not become embittered when an insensitive constituency makes life miserable?

# 9
# Completely Equipped

For several years, I was in charge of maintenance operations for a guest ranch in the Colorado mountains. One of my continuing battles was trying to get the young men who worked with us to use the correct tools for each job. When they didn't, there often was a dual problem—something broken and something unfinished.

"Well," the employee would begin, "I thought I could pull that 30 penny nail with this claw hammer." Result: Broken handle—nail still in place.

"I didn't have the pry bar with me, so I tried to dislodge the rock with my shovel." Result: Broken handle—rock still in place.

"Didn't have a wrench with me, so I tried to loosen the nut with my pliers." Result: Nut still in place with the edges chewed off.

As God's agents of change, we approach each situation with a tool, a method, or a weapon which we believe will turn things around. It is of utmost importance that we understand the tools available to us and also those which we are not free to use.

The spiritual agent of change cannot use the world's methods and expect them to accomplish the work of God. Moses took his first action (killing the Egyptian) based on anger, pride, and self-appointment. He found that instead of establishing himself as Israel's deliverer, his actions knocked him out of the running for 40 years.

Let's consider some of the world's methods that are unacceptable for the Christian agent of change.

# Anger

James wrote, "My dear brothers, take note of this: Everyone should be quick to listen, slow to speak, and slow to become angry, for man's anger does not bring about the righteous life that God desires" (James 1:19-20).

Samuel Butler's old saying has well stated the difficulty of bringing about change through the use of anger: "He that complies against his will, is of his own opinion still." Sitting in the corner and facing the wall, Dennis the Menace personifies the issue as he tells his mother, "I may be sitting down on the outside, but I'm standing up on the inside."

Anger may produce a variety of results. But it is incapable of producing "the righteous life that God desires," either in us or in those with whom we deal.

# Revenge

If our motive for seeking change is based on revenge ("you got me, so I'm going to get you"), from a spiritual perspective we are doomed to fail. Consider again the testimony of the Apostle Paul: "Do not take revenge, my friends, but leave room for God's wrath, for it is written: 'It is Mine to avenge; I will repay,' says the Lord" (Rom. 12:19). In the Book of Hebrews we read, "For we know Him who said, 'It is Mine to avenge; I will repay,' and again, 'The Lord will judge His people' " (Heb. 10:30).

Coping with revenge is difficult because it is such a part of the fabric of our society and of human experience in total. Revenge is a dominant theme in literature, music, and particularly in films. It is curiously interwoven with a sense of fairness and justice. At the afternoon movie matinee it always seemed right when the cowboy in the white hat finally caught up with the one in the black hat and beat the tar out of him. We yelled, whistled, threw popcorn up in the air, and came back the next Saturday for more of the same.

The agent of change who seeks to represent God in the world must make a practice of presenting himself and his motives to Almighty God, for His evaluation. With the psalmist, we need to pray: "Search me, O God, and know my heart; test me and know my anxious thoughts. See if there is any offensive way in me, and lead me in the way everlasting" (Ps. 139:23-24).

Revenge is a communicable disease that more often than not destroys the one carrying it. It is a tool incapable of accomplishing the work of God.

## Pragmatism

The word *whatever* characterizes the attitudes of many Americans toward life today. It is usually spoken in a casual fashion, accompanied by a shrug of the shoulders. It can mean a variety of things: whatever works, whatever feels good, whatever seems right, whatever you think. Basically, it conveys the attitude that whatever works for you is all right.

Fortunately, we Christians can be spared the agony of this trial and error approach to life—if we will follow God's direction. As agents of change, God commands us to operate on the basis of principle, and not expediency.

During his life, Moses learned the lesson of depending on God and following Him. Among his last words to the nation of Israel were these: "Take to heart all the words I have solemnly declared to you this day, so that you may command your children to obey carefully all the words of this law. They are not just idle words for you—*they are your life*. By them you will live long in the land you are crossing the Jordan to possess" (Deut. 32:46-47, italics mine).

As God's change agents, we are not given the option to pragmatically evaluate His truth by whether or not it works. The test of God's truth is in His character, not in our perception of whether God is bringing about our desired results.

## Impatience

Of course you know what a 400-pound parrot says, "Awk, Polly wants a cracker. NOW!" And that's usually how we want our changes to happen. But impatience—like anger, revenge, and pragmatism—won't get the job done for those of us seeking to cooperate with God in bringing about change.

"Wait for the Lord; be strong and take heart and wait for the Lord" (Ps. 27:14). "So do not throw away your confidence; it will be richly rewarded. You need to persevere so that when you have done the will of God, you will receive what He has promised" (Heb. 10:35-36).

When we reach the point where we say, "I've had it! I'm fed up! I just won't put up with this any longer—nothing's happening," perhaps it's time to back off and ask God for a healthy dose of patience.

Exercising patience doesn't mean that we sit quietly while everything collapses around us. But it *does* mean that we act out of deliberation and calculated conviction, rather than impatience.

As a young officer candidate at the U.S. Army Infantry School in Fort Benning, Georgia, I sat transfixed one night as the world in front of me literally went up in smoke. Some 500 of us sat in bleachers and stared out into the darkness to witness a night-fire demonstration, a simulated defense of a Vietnamese village. We were all vitally interested because we knew that in a matter of months, we would be in Vietnam and this would be a reality, not a demonstration.

Over the public address system came the sounds of Oriental music and an announcer's voice that described the advancement of the imaginary enemy forces and the weapons which were being fired in an attempt to halt them. In front of us, red-tipped tracer bullets whined into the blackness, ricocheting skyward in crazy patterns. Artillery rounds, fired from a battery behind us, rattled overhead, exploding downrange with muffled whumps. Low-flying Air Force jets streaked in, setting the night ablaze with canisters of napalm. The summer air was heavy with the smell of cordite, jellied gasoline, and phosphorus.

As the imaginary enemy drew up to the perimeter of the village, the announcer called on the rifle company in its night defense to fire its final protective fire. Every weapon was fired as fast as possible. The roar was deafening and the night turned crimson as a solid stream of tracers ripped into the blackness.

Around me, subdued curses and low whistles expressed the thoughts of those watching: *How could anything possibly live through that withering hail of fire that seemed to blanket every square inch in front of us?* The answer, of course, was that Vietnam was a *two-way* rifle range, and over there in combat the same stuff that was going out would be coming in. Much of the effectiveness of these weapons of violence would be negated in the exchange of fire. It's hard to fire effectively with your head down.

## Ready for Combat

The weapons of anger, revenge, pragmatism, and impatience often generate a retaliation in kind from those on which they are used. When we use these weapons, we find ourselves in a stalemate from a spiritual perspective. What's going out is also coming in.

God has an alternate plan for His representatives:

> For though we live in the world, we do not wage war as the world does. The weapons we fight with are not the weapons of the world. On the contrary, they have divine power to demolish strongholds. We demolish arguments and every pretension that sets itself up against the knowledge of God, and we take captive every thought to make it obedient to Christ (2 Cor. 10:3-5).

When we consider functioning as God's agents of change in our homes, our schools, our jobs, and our communities, what weapons are available to us? The tools must fit the tasks and the weapons must fit the warfare. Paul wrote:

> Finally, be strong in the Lord and in His mighty power. Put on the full armor of God so that you can take your stand against the devil's schemes. For our struggle is not against flesh and blood, but against the rulers, against the authorities, against the powers of this dark world and against the spiritual forces of evil in the heavenly realms. Therefore, put on the full armor of God, so that when the day of evil comes, you may be able to stand your ground, and after you have done everything, to stand (Eph. 6:10-13).

## Spiritual Armor

Let's consider the armor of God, as Paul presented it in Ephesians 6. From this passage, we can draw applications for our task of cooperating with God in His work of change in the world.

**Stand firm then, with the belt of truth buckled around your waist** (v. 14).

As change agents, we must be willing to "do our homework." Jack Webb portrayed Sergeant Friday in television's classic police series, "Dragnet." As he questioned suspects and witnesses, he popularized a phrase that remained in American slang vocabulary for years: "Just the facts, Ma'am, just the facts." Without accurate information about God, about ourselves, and about the situations in which we are seeking to effect change, we may be missing vital parts of our armor.

Jesus Christ Himself claimed to be "the Way and the Truth and the Life" (John 14:6). In His great prayer for His disciples, Jesus petitioned the Father, "Sanctify them by the truth; Your Word is truth" (John 17:17). Through reading the Bible, studying it, memorizing and thinking about it, we expose our minds to the truth of God. This truth, in turn, transforms the way we see others, ourselves, and God. There are new possibilities, new potentials, and a sense of dealing with reality, not hearsay. It is this truth, personified in Jesus Christ, which sets us free.

**. . . with the breastplate of righteousness in place** (Eph. 6:14).

A person will not last long in the arena of change-making without personal integrity and holiness. During a recent political campaign, a television reporter noted that one indication that a candidate was being taken seriously was the number of people digging into his past, trying to uncover a scandal.

An agent of change leaves himself wide open to the scrutiny and criticism of anyone who chooses to take a shot at him. While a spotless past is not a requirement, a current posture of honesty and integrity is a must.

As soon as you begin working to bring about change, you will likely become the target of criticism. While anger and retaliation, mudslinging, and smear campaigns often characterize the world's tactics to counter this kind of situation, God has a different weapon for His people—righteous living.

Live such good lives among the pagans that, though they

> accuse you of doing wrong, they may see your good deeds and glorify God on the day He visits us. . . . For it is God's will that by doing good, you should silence the ignorant talk of foolish men (1 Peter 2:12, 15).

Personal holiness, righteousness, and integrity mean that our lives are the same on the inside as they are on the outside. There is no discrepancy between the way we walk and the way we talk. A change agent who constantly glances over his shoulder to see who is watching has a hard time doing the job at hand.

Another product of righteousness, essential for anyone working to turn things around, is boldness. "The wicked man flees though no one pursues, but the righteous are as bold as a lion" (Prov. 28:1).

The boldness produced by integrity is a liberating factor that frees us to move into areas where we would fear to tread were it not for God's work in our lives. "For God did not give us a spirit of timidity, but a spirit of power, of love, and of self-discipline" (2 Tim. 1:7).

Without integrity, we often persuade others to trust us with tasks which God cannot trust us with. When we try to live two lives and serve two masters we become prisoners of our own sham. We are shackled by our own lack of confidence in our ability or willingness to trust and follow Christ.

> **. . . and with your feet fitted with the readiness that comes from the Gospel of peace** (Eph. 6:15).

When we enter the battle for change we must remember the Source of our marching orders. Jesus Christ Himself calls us to follow Him and make disciples. He calls us to a commitment and lifestyle that will inevitably be at crosscurrents with the society in which we live. But we should not be discouraged when we follow God. "Therefore, since through God's mercy we have this ministry, we do not lose heart" (2 Cor. 4:1).

> **In addition to all this, take up the shield of faith, with which you can extinguish all the flaming arrows of the evil one** (Eph. 6:16).

Through faith we can avoid our natural tendency to approach change through pragmatism and impatience. By faith, we can affirm our conviction that God's methods really are best and that by following them we can accomplish His purposes.

Through my involvement with single adults the past couple of years, I've noticed a curious phenomenon among many divorced persons. They still try to change their ex-spouses. And in most cases, they still try to use the methods that contributed to their marriage break-ups in the first place. Anger, revenge, impatience, and pragmatism have created stalemates. Their continuing relationships, centered mostly around custody and visitation of children, are no better than they were prior to their divorces.

On the other hand, those who adopt the weapons which God has designated for the warfare usually see a dramatic turnaround, mostly in their own attitudes. As they exercise forgiveness and show love to their ex-spouses, and by faith obey God, they experience a confidence and security that had eluded them before.

The only way we as agents of change can positively contribute to healthy changes in the life of another person is to first see that our own lives are centered on the Person of Jesus Christ and ordered according to His Word.

**Take the helmet of salvation** (Eph. 6:17).

Most of us realize that we are never going to "turn around" everything to which we set our hands and hearts. Injustice, inequality, and cruelty will continue even after our efforts stop. But we have assurance from God that a day will come when He will judge the earth and establish a kingdom of righteousness.

We Christians have been accused of having a pie-in-the-sky-by-and-by mentality, of being so heavenly-minded that we are of no earthly good. To offset this, we've neglected the subjects of heaven and the Lord's return. But our faith in Christ gives us eternal hope. We should be reminded that the Apostle Paul, that great first century agent of change, wrote, "If only for this life we have hope in Christ, we are to be pitied more than all men" (1 Cor. 15:19).

The helmet of salvation protects our minds from the enemy's suggestions that we give up, quit, and pack it in since we probably won't accomplish our goals anyway. Our goals are wrapped up within the goals of our heavenly Father who has called us to cooperate with Him in His great program of change, a program which He has promised to bring to completion.

> **. . . and the sword of the Spirit, which is the Word of God** (Eph. 6:17).

> All Scripture is inspired by God and is useful for teaching the faith and correcting error, for resetting the direction of a man's life and training him in good living. The Scriptures are the comprehensive equipment of the man of God, and fit him fully for all branches of his work (2 Tim. 3:16-17, PH).

While some of us might see this as a mandate to simply quote Scripture verses to those with whom we are trying to effect change, there is a deeper and more profound role of the Spirit's sword in our lives. As God's Word is read, studied, preached, shared, and fleshed out in our lives, He uses it to pierce through the barriers of inattention and self-sufficiency in others' lives. In the hands of the Spirit, the sword of God's Word is a multifaceted and effective weapon.

> **And pray in the Spirit on all occasions with all kinds of prayers and requests** (Eph. 6:18).

God's great initiators of change throughout history have been people of prayer. We marvel at accounts of people who rose early in the morning each day to pray. Then we wonder at our own ineffectiveness at changing lives for God.

Moses found himself cast off—a failure in an area where he desperately wanted to succeed. He had fancied himself a deliverer, but found that his human methods disqualified him from becoming part of the solution for his people's problems.

Think for a moment of an area in which you want very much to be used as God's agent of change. How do you plan to go about it? God has comprehensively equipped you with the weapons necessary to wage His warfare of change—a warfare, which unlike the world's, leads not to death, but life.

# STUDY QUESTIONS

1. Based on your consideration of Ephesians 6:10-18, is there a "chink in your armor"? What piece of God's equipment for change are you most likely to neglect in your life?

2. What is your strongest point of God's armor? How can you best use it?

3. Are there any areas of your relationships with others that resemble a "two-way rifle range"? What do you feel is the key to ending the hostilities?

4. Make a note of one area of your life in which you could begin using a new tool—the right one—to do the job this week.

5. Will you make it a point to speak a word of encouragement to someone whom you observe this week doing God's work in God's way?

# 10
# Confronting Opposition

Opposition is inherent in the process of change. We may encounter it in varying degrees of intensity, ranging from mild reluctance to open hostility. Men and women have been snubbed for seeking unpopular political change, arrested for seeking radical social change, and killed for tampering with religion.

Spiritual change has never been popular. Our human tendency is to figure out why we are right just as we are, not why we are wrong in the ways another person points out to us. Yet our Lord said:

> Blessed are you when people insult you, persecute you, and falsely say all kinds of evil against you because of Me. Rejoice and be glad, because great is your reward in heaven, for in the same way they persecuted the prophets who were before you (Matt. 5:11-12).

These words are not a call for change agents to act in offensive ways. They are, rather, a statement of fact that when we seek spiritual change, there will be opposition. But we shouldn't be surprised by it.

## Persecution Is Normal

Several years ago a Bible college professor spoke on the subject of the persecution of Christians. His thesis was that persecution is the norm for the church, rather than the exception. The history of the church shows that people have faced opposition for their beliefs. When we aren't being persecuted for our Christian faith, he suggested that we:

- recognize it as an abnormal situation that could change at any time.
- take advantage of our opportunities of freedom to share the Gospel of Christ freely with others.
- buy up the time to store away great portions of the Bible in our memory, in the event that the Scriptures become unavailable to us.
- help those Christians in other places who *are* facing persecution.

The tenor of his message was not that of an alarmist shouting, "Hurry, before it's too late." Rather, it was the firm testimony of a realist who had spent much time studying both the Scriptures and history. I believe that he was right—in America we are living in an unusual day. Can you imagine how far you would have gotten in first-century Rome with a "Honk if You Love Jesus" bumper sticker on your chariot?

Other aspects of our contemporary world bring us closer to reality. In Uganda and Cambodia, men and women have lost their lives for no other reason than claiming to be followers of Jesus Christ. Today, many Christians walk through the valley of the shadow of death in the ghettos of American cities. Persecution for their faith is much closer than half a world away.

When God spoke with Moses at the burning bush and commissioned his return to Egypt, He told him that Pharaoh would oppose this change from the very beginning. But God assured Moses that His mighty hand of divine power would deliver Israel from its oppressive captivity.

In Exodus, chapters 5—12, we read the account of Moses and Aaron's appearances before Pharaoh—the opposition they encountered, and the work of God in each situation. From this passage come four important principles for all of us to follow as we seek to be agents of spiritual change.

## Know the Message and Stick to It

Seven times Moses said to Pharaoh, "This is what the Lord, the God of Israel says, 'Let My people go, so that they may worship Me.' " There was no confusion about the basic issue in this situation. Moses knew what

God had said and did not dilute it or deviate from it.

In contrast, the Gospel of Jesus Christ in today's world has become a mixed message which is confusing to many. What does it mean to be a Christian? Why does a person need to respond to the invitation of Jesus Christ to accept Him as Saviour and Lord?

Why do we need Jesus Christ? To make us happy or financially successful? In order for us to have good marriages, cope with our problems, or find meaning in our lives? Probably, most people could do all of these things and more without God's help.

We need Jesus Christ to save us from the eternal consequences of our sin, not to make us happy. Certainly a person's decision to become a Christian has a profound effect on every area of life, often transforming previous failure into success, but that is not the primary issue.

In every change for which we work, the primary issue is an individual's personal relationship with Almighty God through Jesus Christ. The Apostle Paul expressed it this way:

> All this is from God who reconciled us to Himself through Christ and gave us the ministry of reconciliation: that God was reconciling the world to Himself in Christ, not counting men's sins against them. And He has committed to us the message of reconciliation. We are therefore Christ's ambassadors, as though God were making His appeal through us. We implore you on Christ's behalf: Be reconciled to God (2 Cor. 5:18-20).

Jesus Christ has not called us to a self-serving gospel of self-fulfillment. He has called us to live out the message that only through faith in His sacrifice on the cross, can we find eternal life. It is because of what He has done that we can stand clean and forgiven, unashamed in God's presence. That is the basic issue of life.

## Perseverance—Stay with It

We often approach the issue of spiritual change with people from a sign-up-or-get-out mentality. If they aren't ready to buy the whole package we're offering, then we want to look for more fertile ground. Unfortunately, we don't always have that option. When we struggle to help our friends, family members, co-workers, and neighbors come to grips with God's claim on their lives, we can't walk away when things don't happen right away. And it's good that we can't.

God could have worked in any number of different ways to deliver His people, but He kept sending Moses back and back to a stubborn ruler whose heart got more obstinate with every visit. The Book of Exodus records 17 separate occasions where Moses appeared to Pharaoh. That seems like a rather inefficient use of manpower for a God who can do anything. Why all the bother, confronting the issue over and over again?

On the surface, the problem seemed to be an economic and political one. The Israelites wanted to leave the serfdom imposed on them in Egypt, leave the country, and find their own destiny as an independent nation. Egypt wasn't about to give up the cheap-labor backbone of their economy. But the problem was more than a secular issue. It was a process of change that mirrors the underlying struggle of our lives today—who is the acknowledged Master of our lives? Who is in charge?

In Exodus chapters 5—12, we notice that Pharaoh "hardened his heart" and that "God hardened Pharaoh's heart." Was God merely using Pharaoh as a puppet, or did Pharaoh have a choice in the matter? The why and how of Pharaoh's hard heart illustrates another dimension of the necessity for perseverance in confronting the opposition. Repeated confrontation reveals the depth of human rebellion against God.

God, in His omniscience, knew the heart of Pharaoh. He knew He was dealing with a man who was predisposed to having his own way, in spite of anything that could be said or demonstrated to the contrary. Pharaoh hardened his own heart in his initial act of saying: "Who is the Lord that I should obey Him and let Israel go?" God hardened Pharaoh's heart by simply giving him more and more opportunities to choose. Each choice, in the face of miraculous evidence, further solidified Pharaoh's stand against God. Like the man "who remains stiff-necked after many rebukes" (Prov. 29:1), Pharaoh was suddenly destroyed without remedy.

Pharaoh never did have a change of heart. He changed his mind a few times when circumstances became unbearable, but his heart remained fixed against God even as he and his soldiers drowned trying to pursue Israel through the Red Sea.

Part of God's continuing dealing with His human creation in its fallen state, is to reveal the depth of man's rebellion against Him. This is no activity for self-righteous people who want to point a finger at others and condemn them. But it is part of the very fabric of those who seek to represent God in their world. God's greatest Agent of Change personified both the necessity and the unpleasantness of this task.

Jesus Christ, by His words and actions, confronted the world with its sinfulness. He said:

> This is the verdict: Light has come into the world, but men loved darkness instead of light because their deeds were evil. . . . If I had not come and spoken to them, they would not be guilty of sin. Now, however, they have no excuse for their sin. He who hates Me hates My Father as well. If I had not done among them what no one else did, they would not be guilty of sin. But now they have seen these miracles, and yet they have hated both Me and My Father (John 3:19; 15:22-24).

As God's agents of change, we must remember, like Moses, that God is in charge of the results. If He chooses that we confront opposition, time after time, with no apparent movement toward our objective, we should remember that revealing the depth of man's sinfulness, and thereby the full extent of God's justice and grace, is part of His continuing work in this world. It is not a popular work, nor is it pleasant, but it is one in which our sovereign Lord may involve us, just as He did His own Son.

## Demonstration of God's Power

From God's perspective, revealed in Exodus 6 and 7, another of His purposes in our confronting opposition is so that He might demonstrate His mighty power, to both unbelievers and believers. Each occasion when Moses and Aaron appeared before Pharaoh marked a new demonstration of God's power in Egypt.

For the Egyptians, the overriding purpose was that they might recognize Jehovah as the one true God. "And the Egyptians will know that I am the Lord when I stretch out My hand against Egypt and bring the Israelites out of it" (Ex. 7:5).

As a result of God's power demonstrated in Egypt, some Egyptians came to believe in Him and obey His Word. Even those in other countries heard and were awed by His power (Josh. 2:8-11).

For the Israelites, those who were already believers, God desired to increase their faith and their sense of His presence and leadership in their lives. "I will take you as My own people, and I will be your God. Then you will know that I am the Lord your God, who brought you out from under the yoke of the Egyptians" (Ex. 6:7).

The principle here is that deep spiritual change only occurs as a result of God's power at work in our lives. Nothing short of the mighty hand of God can draw us in faith to Him. And the method of demonstrating His power is entirely up to Him.

Most of us yearn for more of the spectacular in our efforts to convince others of their need for God. Somehow we reason that if only there were a mighty outpouring of God's power through our lives, in signs and wonders and miracles, that people would believe. But the evidence from Scripture doesn't support this assumption. Supernatural doings seem to accentuate the difference between believers and unbelievers, rather than drawing unbelievers to faith.

Who had the best front row seat for all the miracles in Egypt? Pharaoh. Who didn't believe? What about the people who watched Jesus perform miracles? Scores simply turned and walked away while others accused Him of being in league with the prince of demons. In Jesus' story of the rich man, Lazarus, and Father Abraham (Luke 16:19-31), the rich man begs to have Lazarus sent back from the dead to warn the rich man's brothers to repent. Abraham's reply is: "If they do not listen to Moses and the Prophets, they will not be convinced even if someone rises from the dead" (Luke 16:31).

But God's miraculous power is not demonstrated solely in the spectacular. One evidence of living a life worthy of the Lord and pleasing Him is "being strengthened with all power according to His glorious might so that you may have great endurance and patience, and joyfully [give] thanks" (Col. 1:11-12).

Not spectacular, but definitely miraculous. We have God's promise that His mighty hand will be at work in and through us as His ambassadors in this world.

As we persevere in the battle for spiritual change, His power will strengthen us. To do what? Raise up hoards of frogs on our pagan neighbor's lawn? Turn the water in the local porno king's swimming pool to blood? God *could* do that. Yet we are told that His power will be demonstrated through our lives in terms of great endurance, perseverance, patience, and a joyful thankfulness to God.

Remember the action of Jesus which amazed Pilate? Which miracle was it during the interrogation of our Lord? Which plague upon the Roman soldiers?

> The chief priests accused [Jesus] of many things. So again Pilate asked Him, "Aren't You going to answer? See how many things they are accusing You of?" But Jesus still made no reply, and Pilate was amazed (Mark 15:3-5).

God's plan for bringing about spiritual change may involve our suffering unjustly as we continue to confront opposition for the cause of Christ.

> But if you suffer for doing good and you endure it, this is commendable before God. To this you were called, because Christ suffered for you, leaving you an example, that you should follow in His steps. "He committed no sin, and no deceit was found in His mouth." When they hurled their insults at Him, He did not retaliate; when He suffered, He made no threats. Instead, He entrusted Himself to Him who judges justly (1 Peter 2:20-23).

We are to expect God's demonstration of power in the battle for spiritual change, and we are to trust His choice of methods.

## Prayer

In his confrontation of opposition, Moses continued to take the issues back to God. The dimension of prayer was vital to this man who became known as "the friend of God." When things went wrong, Moses prayed. When victories came, he led the people in songs and prayers of thanksgiving.

In chapter 9 we considered the weapons available to the agent of spiritual change. Paul introduced Ephesians 6 by saying: "For our struggle is not against flesh and blood, but against the rulers, against the authorities, against the powers of this dark world and against the spiritual forces of evil in the heavenly realms" (Eph. 6:12).

As we learn that our battle is indeed a spiritual one, we are thrown toward the weapons which are effective. A rifle is no good against a tank. We would be foolish to attack an armored vehicle with a small-caliber weapon. Yet often we try to bring about spiritual change in a prayerless vacuum.

As you study the lives of God's agents of change in the Scriptures and in the history of the Christian church, you will find them to be people of prayer. E.M. Bounds in his classic booklet, "Power through Prayer" has well said:

> The men who have most fully illustrated Christ in their character, and have most powerfully affected the world for Him, have been men who spent so much time with God as to make it a noticeable feature of their lives.
>
> Prayer is not a little habit pinned on to us while we were tied to our mothers' apron strings; neither is it a little decent quarter of a minute's grace said over an hour's dinner, but it is a most serious work of our most serious years.

As John White has so well noted:

> Prayer is not *you* trying to move *God*. Prayer is among other things *being caught up* into God's directions and activity. He orders the affairs of the universe, and He invites you to participate by prayer. Intercession is God and you in partnership, bringing His perfect plans into being (*The Fight*, Intervarsity, p. 27).

Perhaps the guidance we most need as far as praying goes is simply, "Do it!" We are long on knowledge and short on motivation in this area. Prayer is simply participating with God in effecting change.

God told Moses to go to Pharaoh—possibly the last person Moses wanted to see—and deal with him about turning things around for Israel. As he confronted the opposition to God's plan for His people, Moses had to contend with rejection, counterfeit signs, obstinancy, and broken promises. Yet his perseverance in confronting Pharaoh resulted in the demonstration of God's power in unmistakable ways. He knew the message, he stayed with it, and he undergirded it all with fervent prayer.

# STUDY QUESTIONS

1. Do you find that your greatest opposition to being a Christian agent of change comes from other people, circumstances, or from within yourself?

2. Read 1 Timothy 3:10-13. How would you answer a friend who was living a genuinely Christian life but was worried because he wasn't suffering persecution?

3. Do you believe that Pharaoh had a choice, or that he was a pawn in God's hands? What other portions of Scripture help you arrive at your conclusion?

4. What is your first reaction when you suffer unjustly for something you didn't do, or for something which you believe would benefit those who oppose you?

5. What can you do this week to help you maintain the proper perspective in confronting opposition?

# 11
# Circumstances

In our efforts to affect situations and people around us in positive spiritual ways, we hunger for a solid $1 + 1 = 2$ progression that moves us swiftly toward our goal. Take one Christian who is conscientiously seeking to obey God's teaching, add one action that is biblically correct, and we expect to see some movement toward the goal and some improvement in the circumstances. Unfortunately, that doesn't always happen.

When we take correct action as God's agents of change, things don't always get better. When we see that $1 + 1 = -7$, then we are tempted to question the validity of our proposed change, the soundness of our methods, or perhaps both. The results of Moses' first encounter with Pharaoh should encourage us when circumstances deteriorate after we have done what we believe is the right thing.

## "Who Is the Lord?"

Moses and Aaron appeared before Pharaoh, told him exactly what God had instructed them to say, and things immediately got worse. Exodus 5 and 6 give the account of this cause/effect encounter, and insight into how it fits into the continuing process of functioning as God's agents of change.

In the first place, Pharaoh refused to acknowledge the existence of God. "Who is the Lord, that I should obey Him and let Israel go?" Did you ever try to talk to someone about God who didn't believe in Him? Moses did.

Next, Pharaoh refused to even consider acting on the word of a God he neither knew nor acknowledged. "I do not know the Lord and I will not let Israel go." Have you ever tried to communicate biblical teaching to someone who refused to admit that there was even a possibility the Bible had any connection with divine inspiration and authority? Moses knew a similar frustration.

Next, Pharaoh refused to even dignify Moses' request by linking it to a spiritual issue. *God* says? Not a chance! "Moses and Aaron, why are *you* taking the people away from their labor? Get back to work!" The issue, as far as Pharaoh was concerned, was laziness—not obedience to God.

That same day, Pharaoh issued an order that the Israelites would be required to make the same number of bricks each day that they had in the past, only they would have to gather their own straw. It would not be supplied for them.

When the quota wasn't met, the Israeli foremen were beaten. They, in turn, appealed to Pharaoh who accused them of being lazy and informed them that he would not change the requirement.

When those foremen left Pharaoh's presence, Moses and Aaron were waiting for them. The foremen said, "May the Lord look upon you and judge you! You have made us a stench to Pharaoh and his servants and have put a sword in their hand to kill us" (Ex. 5:21).

Not bad for the first week on the job as a change agent. Pharaoh is mad at you, your own people are mad at you, and circumstances are 100 percent worse than when you started. Is this what you get for obeying God? You wonder if Moses was beginning to think that *he* was the problem. He was batting 0 for 2 in the deliverance department at this point. Was God's method any better than his method 40 years ago? Moses figured that both had resulted in failure.

## Why Obey If It Makes Things Worse?

Moses could have gone a lot of places in his discouragement. He could have hightailed it back to Midian and forgotten the whole thing. He could have retreated inside himself in depression and discouragement. He could have gone back to Pharaoh in anger and tried the same message a little louder. *But Moses went to the Lord*, and right here we find an important principle for our own lives when right action results in difficult circumstances.

> Moses returned to the Lord and said, "O Lord, why have You brought trouble upon this people? Is this why You sent me? Ever since I went to Pharaoh to speak in Your name, he has brought trouble upon this people, and You have not rescued Your people at all" (Ex. 5:22-23).

Moses went to God with his feelings of failure. He also brought with him the plight of the people who were suffering because of his actions. Moses had wanted to deliver the Israelites, to help them, and instead he had harmed them. And to top it all off, God had not rescued His people as He said He would.

The continuing dilemma of a Christian agent of change is, "Why do what's right if it makes things worse? If there is a chance that my actions may cause a bad situation to worsen, why even try to do what I believe God wants me to?" I don't believe this quandary is confined to our push-button age in which we expect our every move to bring about the desired result. It was just as real in Moses' life as it is in ours, and we must learn as he did, to return from setbacks to the presence of God. That is the only place where the problem can be resolved.

A divorced friend of ours recently faced this type of situation. Several months after her divorce, she became aware of her need to acknowledge to her ex-husband how she had contributed to the breakup of their marriage. Through her own personal study of the Bible, discussions with friends, and the gentle urging of God's Spirit within her, she resolved to take this difficult step.

She phoned her ex-husband, shared with him the things which had been weighing her down with guilt, and asked for his forgiveness. He responded by saying: "It's about time you admitted the whole thing was your fault. I've known it all along. And, no, I won't forgive you now or ever for what you did to me."

Now, who needs input like that? Not her. And not you or me. We may feel devastated by an unjust, unconcerned reaction to our best efforts to do what is right. But our feelings of despair are overshadowed by God's sustaining power in our lives as we obey Him. Our friend was amazed at the inner peace she felt in the face of her ex-husband's retaliation.

## God Is Still at Work

When we turn to God for help in the face of unjust response, we find His encouragement to carry on. "Then the Lord said to Moses, 'Now you will see what I will do to Pharaoh: Because of My mighty hand he will let them go; because of My mighty hand he will drive them out of his country' " (Ex. 6:1).

God's promise is that His mighty hand will be at work in our situation. But the only way we will see it is to accept God's promise by faith and carry on in the right direction. "Without faith it is impossible to please God, because anyone who comes to Him must believe that He exists and that He rewards those who earnestly seek Him" (Heb. 11:6).

Faith, for the agent of spiritual change, is not a buzzword to use in church gatherings. It is a necessity for continuing to pursue God-originated goals and methods in the face of adverse circumstances. Faith is the belief that God is God and that He is to be trusted and obeyed no matter what the results may be. If He says that love, forgiveness, kindness, and patience are the right ways to turn a personal relationship or a situation around, then we should continue to use them even when the desired results don't come right away.

Society today says just the opposite: "If an old accepted way of behaving isn't making you happy, abandon it and find something that will. If your marriage relationship isn't satisfying, get out of it." The world puts pressure on all of us to take whatever steps are necessary to make sure we are ecstatically happy.

The world says we should do only "what works," what brings us satisfaction. A popular psychology seminar likens people to rats in a maze, who having found cheese once in the fourth tunnel, will keep going back down the fourth tunnel forever, even when they find no cheese. But this question occurs to me: *What if I believe that it is God who keeps sending me back down that fourth tunnel?*

I don't believe God expects us to put our feelings in a safety deposit box and live without joy and satisfaction. But at the same time, I don't believe God wants us to order our lives and our service for Him exclusively around how we *feel* about things—especially circumstances. If the Scriptures convince us of our need for faith, then our need for patience follows as a corollary. "We do not want you to become lazy, but to imitate those who through faith and patience inherit what has been promised" (Heb. 6:12). "Wait for the Lord; be strong and take heart and wait for the Lord" (Ps. 27:14).

Living in obedience to God's commands means that when we do the right thing, things may not immediately get better, but eventually they get right. That is God's promise.

Right now it is April in Colorado—the time when everyone here wishes it was spring, but it isn't, and it won't be for quite awhile. Several months ago, I planted some bulbs on the east side of our house in anticipation of having some summer flowers in a former bare spot. Right now, that spot looks like it always did, but I'm confident that soon a marvelous change will start taking place. And I expect to get just what I planted.

As you read the following words from the Apostle Paul, try to apply them to the changes you are working toward in your life right now:

> Do not be deceived: God cannot be mocked. A man reaps what he sows. The one who sows to please his sinful nature, from that nature will reap destruction; the one who sows to please the Spirit, from the Spirit will reap eternal life. Let us not become weary in doing good, for at the proper time, we will reap a harvest if we do not give up. Therefore, as we have opportunity, let us do good to all people, especially to those who belong to the family of believers (Gal. 6:7-10).

## Hope for the Discouraged

When Moses sought God in prayer, he received, first, a message to bolster his own faith. God assured Moses of His identity, His trustworthy character, and His concern for Israel. God also reminded Moses of His promise to deliver His people (Ex. 6:2-5).

Then God gave Moses a word to speak to the discouraged nation of Israel:

> Therefore, say to the Israelites, "I am the Lord, and I will bring

you out from under the yoke of the Egyptians. I will free you
from being slaves to them and will redeem you with an outstretched arm and with mighty acts of judgment. I will take you
as My own people, and I will be your God. Then you will know
that I am the Lord your God, who brought you out from under
the yoke of the Egyptians. And I will bring you to the land I
swore with uplifted hand to give to Abraham, to Isaac, and to
Jacob. I will give it to you as a possession. I am the Lord"
(Ex. 6:6-8).

So Moses passed this encouraging message on to his people and, as
you might have suspected, they paid no attention to him. "Moses
reported this to the Israelites, but they did not listen to him because of
their discouragement and cruel bondage" (Ex. 6:9).

When people are still up to their armpits in alligators, it's tough to
convince them that you'll ever get the swamp drained. If you find
yourself working toward change in a leadership capacity, one of your
most difficult tasks will be to keep your people encouraged. I find that
throughout Scripture, there is a pattern which indicates that God encour-
ages leaders and leaders encourage their people. If a leader isn't finding
that encouragement from God, he's going to run out of encouragement
for others in a hurry.

But you don't have to be an up-front, elected, or appointed leader to
engage in the ministry of encouragement. A year before my mother died,
she and Dad decided to leave Oklahoma and move to Colorado Springs.
Quite a decision for a retired couple who had lived in the same city for 40
years. Besides the upheaval of moving, they were facing the grim reality
that Mother was seriously ill and didn't have long to live. Before my
parents left, many people dropped over to say good-bye, and extend their
best wishes. But one man, a dear Christian friend, had a special ministry
to them. Before leaving, he paused, put his arms around both of them,
and said, "Let's just have prayer together before you go."

What a ministry to spend a few moments leading close friends into the
presence of the One who "charms our fears, that bids our sorrows
cease." How often we try to bolster the spirits of those around us with
empty words of hopefulness which skirt both the issue of the concern and

the answer to it: "Well, I sure hope everything works out all right." I'm so grateful that in a moment of my parents' deep need, a man reached out to them with his arms and his heart.

The realization that we will face adverse circumstances in our efforts to bring about change is not negative thinking. It is looking at things realistically and preparing to meet the challenge as informed people. The Apostle Peter wrote that we should prepare our minds for action (1 Peter 1:13).

Toward the end of my army basic training, a young lieutenant who knew I was headed for officer candidate school, sat me down one day and said: "I want to tell you what's going to happen when you get to Fort Benning." He detailed a process of mental, verbal, and physical harrassment that sounded so far-fetched to me that I almost laughed.

I didn't like what I heard about being put under pressure just to see how I'd react. I didn't like the idea of being stretched to the limit mentally and physically, and being around when people who couldn't take it "snapped." But I listened. When I got there and it happened just as he said, it was encouraging to know that others had been there and had made it through.

As we work in partnership with God for change, we have every reason to be optimistic about our calling and what is ahead. At the same time, our optimism should be balanced with realism growing out of the teaching and examples of Scripture.

## Living by Faith

I love the 11th chapter of Hebrews, the Bible's hall of fame, where people are commended for their faith. We read of Noah, Abraham, Moses, and many others "who through faith conquered kingdoms, administered justice, and gained what was promised; who shut the mouths of lions, quenched the fury of the flames, and escaped the edge of the sword; whose weakness was turned to strength, and who became powerful in battle and routed foreign armies. Women received back their dead, raised to life again" (Heb. 11:33-35).

But the chapter goes on to include another group of people who are also commended for their faith.

Others were tortured and refused to be released, so that they

might gain a better resurrection. Some faced jeers and flog-
ging, while still others were chained and put in prison. They
were stoned; they were sawed in two; they were put to death by
the sword. They went about in sheepskins and goatskins,
destitute, persecuted, and mistreated—the world was not
worthy of them. They wandered in deserts and mountains, and
in caves and holes in the ground (Heb. 11:35-38).

But they were *all* commended for their faith! For some of them, doing
the right thing brought spectacular changes in their circumstances, miraculous deliverances, and stunning reversals in impossible situations.
But others lost their homes and their money, were imprisoned, or were
killed. The obvious conclusion is that the same options of miraculous
deliverance or losing it all exist for us as God's agents of change today, as
we follow God's commands by faith.

How can optimism exist in the face of that kind of realism? I believe it
can by simply looking at what we know and don't know about the future.
When we follow God's directions, here is first of all, what we don't
know:

- We don't know that circumstances will get better. They may get
  worse, a lot worse.
- We don't know that we will ever see the change come to pass
  which we seek to implement. God has called us to be part of a
  process and the results are in His hands.
- We don't know that people will applaud or favorably recognize
  our efforts.

On the other hand, here is what we *do* know:

- We know that Jesus will never leave us or forsake us. If we are
  seeking to genuinely represent Him in our world, then the promise
  of His presence is a resource of great value.
- We know that His sustaining power will undergird and strengthen
  us as we follow Him.
- We know that the results are in His hands. One day, Jesus Christ
  will judge the world in perfect righteousness and justice, resolve
  all conflicts, punish all wrong, and bring peace. As joint heirs,

and as those who will reign with Him, we cannot fail if we cooperate with Him in effecting changes.

# STUDY QUESTIONS

1. What other examples from the Bible can you give of people who did what was right, followed God's commands, and experienced a worsening of circumstances?

2. What do we usually tell ourselves when we follow a certain course of action and things get worse?

3. What parallels can you draw between farming and being an agent of change?

4. As a separate study, consider the plagues of Egypt from Exodus, chapters 5—12. How many of them affected the Hebrews just as they did the Egyptians? What were the results of the plagues in the life of Pharaoh and his court?

5. How has this chapter affected your expectations in the area of working for change? How will it make a difference next time when you obey God, and things get worse?

# 12
# Chronology: Time and the Agent of Change

As I write this, I am sitting in a waiting room outside the intensive care unit of an Oklahoma City hospital. Inside, my father is battling back after a six-hour operation to remove a malignant tumor from his neck. Around me, in the waiting room, a cross section of humanity is engaged in the same activity—waiting.

The telephone rings constantly as friends and relatives call to inquire about those in intensive care. We answer them using a surprisingly similar vocabulary. The most commonly repeated phrase is, "Well, it's just a matter of time." Whether the result is death or life, it's a matter of time. We heal and die in a succession of moments. Long, sometimes seemingly endless moments.

Change seldom happens suddenly. Most "overnight success" stories and "sudden tragedies" are the results of moments, days, and years. The bright new singing star may have spent 10 years as a studio musician, making others sound good. The alcoholic who "lost it all" did so one day at a time. The members of the Chicago Symphony didn't acquire their skills by answering an "Amaze Your Friends in 10 Days" ad in the back of a popular magazine. And as Christians, our own lives and the situations we seek to change seldom turn around overnight.

Perhaps the most familiar summary of Moses' life is the one attributed to the late Dwight L. Moody, who said:

Moses spent 40 years thinking he was somebody
40 years learning he was nobody
40 years discovering what God can do with a nobody.

In one sense, Moses spent all of his life waiting for things to happen. For a long time, he was waiting for his own preparation as an agent of change. Then he waited for God's proper time to take action. And finally, he waited for the response of others to God's commands. I believe that we experience the same three waiting processes in our lives.

# Waiting for Our Own Preparation

Some years back, a major bus company built an entire advertising campaign around the slogan: "Getting There Is Half the Fun." Unfortunately, we don't believe that. "Getting there," in our minds, is a necessary evil and the real joy is found in the destination. That mindset is probably why most of us get extremely frustrated when things don't move along at the rapid pace we would like to see.

One of the most helpful books I have ever read on this subject is *The Adventure of Living* by Dr. Paul Tournier. He expresses the idea that life itself, in *all* its parts, should and can be a great adventure. However, he also adds, "There are people who go on indefinitely preparing for life instead of living it" (Harper and Row).

While the understandable desire of our hearts is that change would hurry up and happen, we also need to slow down and learn to enjoy, or at least appreciate the process. This thought is beautifully expressed by this verse:

Slow me down, Lord. Ease the pounding of my heart by the quieting of my mind. Steady my hurried pace with a vision of the eternal reach of time. Give me, amid the confusion of the day, the calmness of the everlasting hills. Break the tensions of my nerves and muscles with the soothing music of the singing streams that live in my memory. Help me to know the magical restoring power of sleep. Teach me the art of taking minute vacations—of slowing down to look at a flower, to chat with a friend, to pat a dog, to read a few lines from a good book.

> Slow me down, Lord, and inspire me to send my roots deep
> into the soul of life's enduring values that I may grow toward
> the stars of my greater destiny.
>
> (Author unknown)

Slowing down is just the beginning of recognizing and particpating in God's process of preparing us to be His partners in change. Another part of the process is the development of our perseverance. Romans 5:5 is a tremendous verse for change agents: "And hope does not disappoint us, because God has poured out His love into our hearts by the Holy Spirit, whom He has given us."

However, that verse refers to the end product of a process which most of us would rather avoid. It begins in verses 1 and 2 where Paul reminds us that we stand righteous before God and enjoy His peace because of our faith in Christ. As a result, we rejoice in the hope of the glory of God.

But then in verse 3, he outlines the process of further developing the quality of hope in our lives. "Not only so, but we also rejoice in our sufferings, because we know that suffering produces perseverance."

Perseverance means continuing in the face of oppposition. Perseverance cannot be developed in an easy chair. It is something that grows out of a decision to continue when circumstances and our feelings scream at us to quit.

Bryan Allen, a 26-year-old Californian, flew the first man-powered airplane across the English Channel in June 1979. The pedal-powered *Gossamer Albatross* earned Allen and the aircraft's designer, Dr. Paul McCready, a $200,000 prize. But there's a story behind the story.

For six months before the flight, Allen worked out relentlessly on a stationary bicycle, sitting there pedaling for hours, moving nowhere with nothing to look at. But during the flight, when he was exhausted and ready to give up, he didn't. His training paid off.

God's training program for His agents of change is no less demanding.

> Consider it pure joy, my brothers, whenever you face trials of
> many kinds, because you know that the testing of your faith
> develops perseverance. Perseverance must finish its work so
> that you may be mature and complete, not lacking anything
> (James 1:2-4).

God's training through trial may not be pleasant, but it pays off. Perseverance produces character. Character is what we are when the lights are out, when no one is looking, when no one is around who knows us or cares. It is what we do when we have the chance to do anything we want.

## Character Building

Many people have no doubts about what *God* can do in His power, but they are filled with doubts about their own willingness or ability to choose His way in the face of temptation. When we persevere in choosing God's way at times when there is no other good reason to do so except that He has commanded us to follow Him, the product is integrity and character. Character produces hope.

Character, the individual moral and spiritual dimension of our lives, is wrapped up in the ability to say yes and no. As our choosing power is strengthened through suffering to say yes to what is right and no to what is wrong, the resulting character development produces hope for the future. There is hope that no matter what comes along, we will seek God's strength to handle it.

Suffering puts choices into proper perspective. It separates the trivial from the significant in living. As Dr. Richard C. Halverson has said: "Suffering is the 'stuff' of human greatness—it sweeps the shallowness out of life. The man who lives for a cause worthy enough to die for makes suffering serve him—serve his high purpose. And suffering becomes a bonafide asset" (*Perspective*, April 12, 1978).

Perseverance teaches us that we can go through things which we thought would destroy us. As we add one correct choice to another, even when we are relentlessly pulled to yield to temptation, go our own way, and "turn back to Egypt," we discover new experiences of God's power in us.

Character produces the hope and optimism needed by every agent of change. Real character has chosen the right thing when it could have chosen anything and only God would have known. Far from being proud, the person who possesses character humbly relies on God to continue to be faithful in every situation as He has in the past. And that produces hope.

# God's Timetable

One of my favorite jobs while working at a Colorado guest ranch was meeting people at the Denver airport and driving them to the ranch. Everyone always had a million questions and it was fun to whet their appetites for a western vacation by answering all that I could. The kids wanted to know how many horses we had, what their names were, and if they could feed the horses carrots. Mom wanted to know if the kids really would be supervised most of the day and Dad tried to figure out how long it would take us to get there.

Often, Dad would ask how far it was from the airport to the ranch. I would answer, "70 miles." With that figure in mind, he would calculate that the ride would take a little over an hour. The problem is that flatland timetables don't work in the mountains. Those 70 miles would take us two hours to drive.

The route included everything from Interstate 70 to U.S. Forest Service Road #580 which, in places, was only one lane wide. Obviously the rate of travel varied widely from one road to the next. But for a person who had just covered the 1,000 miles between Chicago and Denver in two hours, those next two hours to make 70 miles on the ground seemed interminable.

As God's agents of change, one of our deepest struggles is with *His* timetable. God's timetable doesn't always fit our idea of how long it should take to get from one point to another.

Jesus' disciples illustrate our human preoccupation with *when*, *how many times*, and *how long*. Peter wanted to know how many times he should forgive his brother. As many as seven times? (Matt. 18:21) After Jesus had spoken about the end of the age, His disciples came to Him privately and asked, "When will this happen, and what will be the sign of Your coming and of the end of the age?" (Matt. 24:3)

In fact, the last question they asked Jesus before His ascension was, "Lord, are You at this time going to restore the kingdom to Israel?" (Acts 1:6)

God's timetable is never given to us ahead of time, in familiar measurable increments. Instead, we learn that it is wrapped up in the very nature of God Himself, the One who said "I AM." The One to whom a day is as a thousand years and a thousand years as a day. The same One Peter describes by saying, "The Lord is not slow in keeping His promise, as some understand slowness" (2 Peter 3:9).

How can we understand the timetable of a God who arrives too late to save Lazarus from dying, yet raises him from the dead (John 11); who was born too late to save His people from great suffering at the hand of their enemies; who was born too soon for us to see His human presence, yet was born right on schedule, "when the time had fully come"? (Gal. 4:4) I don't pretend to have a handle on the "how long" and "when" of God's actions. All I know is that God usually takes longer than I would like for the changes I seek to take place.

I have my own little progression figured out when it comes to my role as a change agent. I'm willing to spend some time in preparation; then I expect to move right into the execution of the task. When it is successfully completed, I plan to rest. But God's schedule doesn't always mesh with mine. I struggle to understand the timetable of an all-knowing, timeless God, from my limited, clock-bound perspective. Why can't I figure it out? Why does it seem that I'm always waiting for the right time for God to move?

I believe we often try to impose "flatland timetables" on the work of a God who can move mountains, but in His time. Our challenge is to fit into His timetable for change.

## Dealing with Delays

Next, we spend a great deal of time waiting for other people to respond to the work of God in their lives. We cannot presume to say what the original divine schedule was for Israel's journey from Egypt to Canaan. We do know from Scripture (Deut. 1:2), that by one route, the journey could have been made in 11 days. Instead, due to the rebellion of the people, it took 40 years. Again, this disappointing turn of events forces us to look at the *process* of change, rather than merely at the intended result.

Moses never asked to be the scoutmaster on a 40-year camping trip, but as a result of Israel's disobedience, that's the job he got. With their deliverance from Egypt secured and the miracle at the Red Sea behind them, it would have seemed simple to move right on toward Canaan. But the people rebelled against God and those plans went on the shelf.

How do we react when God's timetable seems to be disrupted by human failure? Can it actually happen? Can the God of Creation delay His plan by people's refusal to cooperate with Him? It seems paradoxical that Almighty God has so limited Himself with respect to His human creation, but the pages of Scripture and our experience bear out this truth (See Num. 14:29-34; Ps. 107:10-12; Matt. 23:37-38). Many a parent has faced the agony of waiting for a child who has gone off on his own willful way, knowing there is no set time that he will return. In the same way, God has given us the freedom to make choices—and He does not override our choices by forcing His will on us.

But no matter the sources of delay in our lives or the lives of those we love, our trust should remain centered in God. He is the One who can take a 13-year delay in the life of Joseph and use it for His glory.

Turn to Genesis 37—50 and reread the fascinating account of the delays in the life of a man whom God used as a significant agent of change. Joseph was sold into slavery by his brothers, falsely accused by a woman, unjustly punished by his employer, and forgotten by a friend. Each action seemed to delay his deliverance by years. Yet God was with Joseph in all of it, preparing him for the day in which he would be thrust into a position of leadership and authority.

While we wait for others to respond to God's work in their lives, we may inherit the results of their obstinancy and human failure. Yet, there is nothing which God cannot turn into an event for our good and His glory. With Him nothing is wasted.

## Creative Waiting

As we work toward spiritual change, what can we expect from God during our waiting days?

*We can expect to be built up and not worn down.* "Wait for the Lord; be strong and take heart and wait for the Lord" (Ps. 27:14). "But those who hope in the Lord will renew their strength. They will soar on wings like eagles; they will run and not grow weary; they will walk and not be faint" (Isa. 40:31).

Waiting for God to move in a certain situation is another part of cooperating with Him in change. It is a wait that confidently anticipates His action at the time when He knows it will be correct and most effective. By faith, we can expect His strength to undergird us during difficult waiting days.

*We can expect to discover patience as a learned quality.* The only situations in which we can learn patience are those which normally would cause us to become impatient. Patience in the course of daily living is a quality which we expect to develop with physical and mental maturity. Adults are expected to be more patient than children. But patience with God as He deals in our lives and the lives of those we love is a learned quality associated with spiritual maturity.

*We can expect to wait actively and creatively.* Waiting for God is not like waiting for a bus. We do not suspend all activity, sit down somewhere, and wait for God to come along and intervene. Someone has said that all things come to those who hustle while they wait.

What was Moses doing as he waited for God to deliver His people from Egypt? Was he sitting in the sand, staring at the sky? No, he was actively involved in obeying God. He was confronting Pharaoh with the issue at hand. He was dealing with the elders of Israel and the people as they reacted to unfavorable circumstances, and he was constantly coming back to God in prayer and in deep need. It was all part of the active process of waiting.

In some situations, our helplessness is more apparent than in others. Often, there seems little we can do while waiting in a hospital for a loved one. When people have scorned our efforts to share the love of God with them, we are forced to back off.

The challenge is to wait actively and creatively without going beyond what God wants us to do. While Abraham was waiting for God to give him an heir through his wife, Sarah, he got a little too creative and fathered a son through Hagar, Sarah's handmaiden (Gen. 16:1-4). In his efforts to help God fulfill His promise, Abraham violated what God wanted. As we seek to wait actively and creatively, the Scriptures and the presence of God's Holy Spirit within us must be our guides during waiting days.

## Time: Minutes or Moments?

I believe there are two final keys which we, as God's agents of change, must employ as we wait.

• *We must begin to live in terms of the calendar, not the stopwatch.*
Several years ago, I read a statement in the "Christian Leadership
Letter" which has stayed with me. In essence, the author said that we
greatly overestimate what we can accomplish in one year and greatly
underestimate what we can accomplish in five. Change—deep, meaningful, lasting change—simply takes time and we must be willing to
approach it that way.

During her short lifetime, writer Flannery O'Connor was widely
misunderstood and criticized for her stories. Her tales, which were often
bloody and violent, did deal with spiritual issues. But many people
denounced her stories in the name of decency and religion. Only since her
death in 1965, have many people realized what Miss O'Connor was
trying to say in her writings. But Flannery O'Connor really didn't care if
people figured her out while she was alive or not. She was quoted as
saying:

> I'm so convinced that what I'm doing is right, I can wait a
> hundred years for the world to discover it.

Can we say the same thing about the changes we are trying to make?

• *We must learn how to "collect our moments."* In terms of money
and influence on the television industry, Norman Lear was undoubtedly
the most successful producer of the 1970s. The creator of Archie Bunker
brought comedy as well as controversy to the nation's television screens.
Lear's library of syndicated shows alone is worth an estimated $200
million.

Yet this man has an interesting concept of success. In an interview for
*Parade* magazine, Mr. Lear said:

> Success is how you collect your minutes. Life is made of small
> pleasures. Good eye contact over the breakfast table with your
> wife. A moment of touching with a friend. Happiness is made
> of those tiny successes. The big ones come too infrequently. If
> you don't have all of those zillions of tiny successes, the big
> ones don't mean anything (Marguerite Michaels, "What'll He
> Do for an Encore?" *Parade*, September 23, 1979, p. 5).

I believe there is much for us to learn from these words. Often we who desire to be agents of change work so hard to accomplish our goals, even worthy spiritual goals, that our lives suffer in the process. God does not intend for us to be "successful" as His representatives at the cost of our marriages, our children, our relationships with parents, brothers, and sisters. If there is a cost to be paid on the part of our families as we follow Jesus Christ, then let it be that they misunderstood our calling, not that we neglected them in the process.

At the end of his life, Moses prayed his great prayer, recorded for us in Psalm 90. He made this request of God: "Teach us to number our days aright, that we may gain a heart of wisdom" (v. 12). Teach us to collect our moments, so that we may become wise.

As agents of spiritual change, we must realize that we will discover God's timetable only if we commit ourselves to Him and take part in the process through which He trains and uses us. Waiting days are growing days, and even delays brought on by human failure can be turned into events which ultimately bring glory to God. And we have need of patience, that after we have done the will of God, we might receive the promise (Heb. 10:36).

# STUDY QUESTIONS

1. When is waiting most difficult for you?

2. What helps you experience the presence of God in your life, even during times of waiting?

3. When you read in Psalm 27:14, "Wait for the Lord," what does that mean to you?

4. List several specific things you can do while you are waiting and working toward a certain change.

5. What should you do when you inherit the unfavorable effects of someone else's failure or disobedience to God?

# 13
# Changing Roles

Will Rogers set for himself the personal goal of becoming the best trick roper in the world. He devoted hours of intense, diligent practice to his craft of making a lariat do unusual things. As part of his act, he developed a light banter which audiences responded to heartily. After awhile, people began to come to hear what Will Rogers had to say, not to watch him do rope tricks.

Rogers adapted his act and made his comments the focus. He changed his role to meet the needs at hand. His willingness to do so enabled him to become one of the most loved- and listened-to figures in American history. Somewhere today is the greatest trick roper in the world. You probably don't know who it is, and I certainly don't. That's what Will Rogers might have been if he had not been willing to change roles.

## Moses' New Job

In our efforts to bring about change, the accomplishment of one goal often signals the beginning of a new challenge that requires us to adapt and change in order to meet it. Accomplished objectives close doors behind us, but leave us looking for new doors which lead to other things. Sometimes we must move in an entirely new direction, but most often, our new roles grow out of our old ones.

Moses was commissioned to lead Israel *out* of Egypt and *into* the

Promised Land. The deliverance of the Hebrew people found him with a continuing responsibility, but also with a change in roles. Moses went from being a revolutionary to an administrator. From his role as a deliverer, he moved on to become a governor. From one who opposed "the Egyptian establishment," he became the head of a new order. He didn't ask for the new job, but he got it anyway.

In Egypt, Moses' main job had been to represent God before Pharaoh, to set forth the demands of the Almighty, and to get the people of Israel out of their bondage. All his energy had been focused on those objectives. But with the Exodus underway, Moses became a leader, a provider, a law-giver, and the main man in charge of complaints.

Backed up against the Red Sea with Pharaoh closing in for the kill? "It's Moses' fault! He got us into this. We were happy where we were."

No water? "Complain to the man in charge. He shouldn't have led us out here if he didn't know where the water holes were."

A dispute over property or a wrong done by a neighbor? "Take it to Moses. Let him decide what to do."

Wondering why Moses, Aaron, and a select few are the ones in charge? Think you can do just as good a job? "Let's get together and challenge his authority. Let's just see who has the right to lead here."

## Prayer and Dependence on God

Moses went from the frying pan into the fire in his new role of leading an unruly multitude on their trek toward Canaan. Yet three lessons from his life stand out as we consider the life of a Christian change agent during a change of roles.

First, *we never outgrow the need for prayer and dependence on God*. It is a curious human trait that we quickly forget how we got where we are. Success is often more difficult to handle than failure, because success leads us to think that we did it on our own. It is a sound axiom of life that "failure is seldom fatal, and success is never final." Success in one role guarantees nothing about the next job down the road.

From Moses' life, we get a sense of a man who knew the reason for his past success, and who knew where to get help for the things ahead:

• Exodus 5:22-23—Moses prayed when circumstances deteriorated after his initial confrontation with Pharaoh.

- Exodus 15:1-19—Moses taught Israel a song of praise to the God who had miraculously delivered them at the Red Sea.
- Exodus 15:22-25—Moses cried out to God to meet their need for water.
- Exodus 32:11—Moses sought the forgiveness of God for the people who rebelled and worshiped the golden calf.

We may reason that Moses had no other recourse than to pray, since his leadership role consisted mostly of meeting one crisis after another with a people who seemed bent on rebellion and self-destruction. But prayer kept him on the job. Moses' overwhelming burden of responsibility, rather than driving him to insanity or back to the ''simple life'' herding sheep in Midian, drove him into a deeper dependence on the power and strength of God.

Moses was also well aware of what could happen when a plateau of success was reached and the burden was lifted. Just before Israel entered the Promised Land, Moses gave them this warning:

> Be careful that you do not forget the Lord, your God, failing to observe His commands, His laws, and His decrees that I am giving you this day. Otherwise, when you eat and are satisfied, when you build fine houses and settle down, and when your herds and flocks grow large and your silver and gold increase and all you have is multiplied, then your heart will become proud and you will forget the Lord your God, who brought you out of Egypt, out of the land of slavery (Deut. 8:11-14).

A profound sense of our need to pray about every situation and to depend on God's wisdom and power is essential as we move from one role to the next in our adventure of making change happen.

## Advice from Others

A second lesson we learn from Moses is that of *being humble enough to accept advice from others.*

One summer day, while working at the guest ranch, I was given the responsibility of digging up an old water line, the exact location of which was unknown. With some knowledge of where it started and where it went, I began digging a trench, hoping to strike the line.

Since I was digging in a central area, people were constantly walking by, asking what I was doing, asking if I'd found it yet, and offering suggestions on where and how I should dig. By late afternoon, I had developed an unspoken philosophy: "I accept advice only from people with shovels in their hands." If people weren't willing to get in the trench and dig with me, I wasn't interested in what they had to say.

Now that may be a typical human attitude, but it caused me to take more time and effort than was necessary to find that pipe. Many of those people wandering by were successful businessmen who knew a lot more about thinking and problem-solving than I did. My own stubbornness and pride were hindrances to success in that case. When I finally took the advice of one man, whom I later learned was in the construction business, I found the pipe in a matter of minutes. Change agents must be learners, and it often takes sensitivity and humility to respond to the sound suggestions of those around us.

By accepting the advice of his father-in-law, Jethro, Moses began *overcoming the myth of indispensability*. Jethro helped Moses come to grips with his need to delegate authority and responsibility to others, in order to better meet the needs of the people (Ex. 18:13-26). A person who insists on "doing it all himself" may never get it all done. Perhaps merely a portion of it will get done, and that only marginally.

The *Australian Women's Weekly* recently carried a story titled, "How I Stopped Being a Nag and Became a Home Administrator." It was the story of a young mother, suddenly a single parent and working again, who realized that the only way she could survive was to share her household duties with her children and help them learn to accept responsibility. A Christian agent of change, in a leadership role, faces a similar need.

While Moses was leading Israel, he was also training his replacement. An important undercurrent in the life of Moses was his relationship with his young aide, Joshua. Joshua, involved in the very heartbeat of Israel's deliverance and wilderness leadership, learned his lessons from long association with the man who knew God, face-to-face. More than simply acquiring the mechanics of management, Joshua caught the vision of leading a people in the service of God.

Valuable, but not indispensable; leading, yet training others to assume that role; giving, yet accepting the help of others. These are the challenges of changing roles.

## A Sense of History

We also learn from Moses' experience, *the importance of having a sense of history.*

The college course that gave me the most difficulty was called, "Political Parties and Pressure Groups." It was taught by a professor who was over 65 years old and the class was full of retired Air Force officers. The professor and those men talked about Hoover, Roosevelt, Truman, and Eisenhower as if they were old friends. They reminisced about everything from the Great Depression to the McCarthy Communist purges of the 1950s. I nearly flunked the course because I didn't have the faintest idea what they were talking about. For me, it was a course in history. For them, it was a walk down memory lane.

Years later, I remember being astounded when not one student in my junior high class could tell me anything about John F. Kennedy. Then it occurred to me that when Kennedy was assassinated in 1963, I was a junior in college and my present students weren't even born yet. My experience was their history.

And now consider the problem of Moses. He began with a generation of people who had experienced the hardships of Egypt, and had seen God perform miracles in their behalf. God struck dead the firstborn of the Egyptians in order to free Israel. He parted the Red Sea for them and destroyed their Egyptian pursuers in its waters. He provided water from a rock, manna from thin air, and guidance from a pillar of cloud that moved before them. Yet that rebellious and unbelieving generation was condemned to die wandering in the wilderness. Their children would be the ones to possess Canaan (Num. 14:20-35).

I wonder what they talked about for 40 years as they made camp, broke camp, and made camp again. I wonder what the parents said to their children as they grew up and what the children thought as they became adults and watched an entire generation of fighting men die without ever battling to possess their promised inheritance. Feasts and festivals brought to mind a call from God that had been placed "on hold" till the hard hearts of one generation gave way to the willingness of the next. Remembering and studying the past are essential as we participate with God in His work in the world.

Our challenge, as agents of change, is to develop within ourselves and the lives of others, a sense of where we have come from and where we are going as Christians, both collectively and individually. Having a sense of our collective history does not lock us into the past wishing for "the good old days." Instead, it helps us interpret the events of today and plan for tomorrow.

A political analyst criticized the failure of a U.S. president to properly handle foreign policy decisions by saying of him, "He has no sense of history." Knowing what the pioneers of our faith have faced in days gone by helps us understand our situation today and provides us with examples to follow and mistakes to avoid. Heresy in the faith tends to repeat itself and we can often unmask modern false doctrines by knowing the fallacies of the past.

On the personal level, a sense of our spiritual history includes the continuing awareness of what God has done for us in the person of Jesus Christ. The Book of Deuteronomy is an excellent guide for developing that personal sense of history in our own lives.

Throughout Deuteronomy, a similar theme is stated over and over: "Remember that you were slaves in Egypt." In Scripture, Egypt is often used to symbolically picture the life of a person before he placed his faith in Jesus Christ. It is a life characterized by the oppression and captivity of sin. It took nothing short of the power of God to deliver us from our own personal Egypt.

Then why, like the liberated nation of Israel, do we keep wanting to go back? Why do the things that characterized our life before we acknowledged Christ as our Lord still hold such a strong attraction for us? Perhaps it's because we don't remember that we were *slaves* in Egypt. We recall the good days and the fun times and forget the bitterness and discouragement that motivated us to seek our Creator and His deliverance. Our memories paint a distorted picture of our former lives.

The Apostle Peter wrote, "For you know that it was not with perishable things such as silver or gold that you were redeemed from the empty way of life, handed down to you from your forefathers, but with the precious blood of Christ, a Lamb without blemish or defect'' (1 Peter 1:18-19).

A continuing sense of our own personal spiritual history keeps us humble in the eyes of God who has brought us "out from Egypt" by His mighty power. It is also necessary to keep us from longing for things in the past, that in fact, never were. Like the nation of Israel, we long to return to Egypt only when we forget that we were slaves there.

## The Greatest Role Change Of All

Perhaps one of the greatest role changes we ever experience is that of becoming *Christian* agents of change in the first place. We move from being rebellious subjects to being ambassadors for the King Himself. Unfortunately, becoming ambassadors often causes us to lose touch with the people to whom we are sent. Instead of getting out with the rebellious subjects, we prefer to remain inside the court and discuss things with other ambassadors.

In an article titled, "The Mint-Flavored Oasis" (*HIS*, April 1980), Joe N. McKeever likened Christians today to an organization named "Desert Dwellers Who Have Found the Water." Their purpose was to meet every week, talk about how they came to the water, and drink. They were only mildly disturbed that people all around the oasis were dying of thirst.

The challenge of an agent of spiritual change is to stand in the gap between man and God, and bring the two together. In order to do that, the change agent must intimately understand both the heart of God and the hearts of people without Him. He must walk and talk both with the Almighty, and with men and women who do not know or care about Him. It takes a concerted effort to do both.

The late Dr. Sam Shoemaker, a canon in the Episcopal church, wrote the following apologia for his life:

So I Stay Near the Door

I stay near the door. I neither go too far in, nor stay too far out, the door is the most important door in the world—it is the door through which men walk when they find God. There's no use my going way inside, and staying there when so many are still outside and they, as much as I, crave to know where the door is. And all that so many ever find is only the wall where a door ought to be. They creep along the wall like blind men, with outstretched, groping hands, feeling for a door, knowing there must be a door, yet they never find it . . . so I stay near the door.

The most tremendous thing in the world is for men to find that door—the door to God. The most important thing any man can do is to take hold of one of those blind, groping hands, and to put it on the latch—the latch that only clicks and opens to the man's own touch. Men die outside the door, as starving beggars die on cold nights in cruel cities in the dead of winter—die for want of what is within their grasp. They live, on the other side of it—live because they have found it. Nothing else matters compared to helping them find it, and open it, and walk in, and find Him . . . so I stay near the door.

Go in, great saints, go all the way in—go way down into the cavernous cellars, and way up into the spacious attics—it is a vast, roomy house, this house where God is. Go into the deepest of hidden casements, of withdrawal, of silence, of sainthood. Some must inhabit those inner rooms, and know the depths and heights of God, and call outside to the rest of us how wonderful it is. Sometimes I take a deeper look in, sometimes venture in a little farther; but my place seems closer to the opening . . . so I stay near the door.

There is another reason why I stay there. Some people get part way in and become afraid lest God and the zeal of His house devour them; for God is so very great, and asks all of us. And these people feel a cosmic claustrophobia, and want to get out. "Let me out!" they cry. And the people way inside only terrify them more. Somebody must be by the door to tell them that they are spoiled for the old life, they have seen too much: once they taste God, nothing but God will do anymore. Somebody must be watching for the frightened who seek to sneak out just where they came in, to tell them how much better it is inside. The people too far in do not see how near these are to leaving— preoccupied with the wonder of it all. Somebody must watch for those who have entered the door, but would like to run away. So for them too I stay near the door.

I admire the people who go way in. But I wish they would not forget how it was before they got in. Then they would be able to help the people who have not yet even found the door, or the people who want to run away again from God. You can go in too deeply, and stay in too long, and forget the people outside the door. As for me, I shall take my old accustomed place, near enough to God to hear Him, and know He is there, but not so far from men as not to hear them, and remember they are there too. Where? Outside the door—thousands of them, millions of them. But—more important for me—one of them, two of them, ten of them, whose hands I am intended to put on the latch. So I shall stay by the door and wait for those who seek it. "I had rather be a doorkeeper . . ." So I stay near the door (*Extraordinary Living For Ordinary Men*, Pyramid Books, pp. 140-142).

As God's agents of change, our roles will change and in order to successfully meet the challenge of change, we will have to adapt while keeping our spiritual bearings. We will never outgrow our needs for prayer and dependence on God. In humility, we can learn from the lives and suggestions of others. And with a growing sense of history, we can carry on the ministry of reconciliation between God and man as we "stay near the door."

# STUDY QUESTIONS

1. Are you facing a role change right now in your life? What indications do you have that God is the moving force bringing about this change?

2. List some of the difficulties we face in handling both failure and success in our lives. Are they different? Which is most difficult for you?

3. In what role do you consider yourself to be indispensable? How do we achieve the proper balance between seeing ourselves as valuable, yet replacable?

4. How and where could you be investing your life in the training of a "Joshua" to carry on your vision?

5. What are you doing to develop a sense of history?

# 14
# Consummation

*Sunday, January 8, 1956, 4:30 P.M.:* Marj Saint waited expectantly next to her radio at a missionary outpost in Ecuador. Her husband, Nate, and four other young men were camped along the Curaray River, seeking to make contact with a Stone-age tribe of South American Indians, the Aucas. The time for their radio check passed by in silence.

*Monday, January 9:* A Missionary Aviation Fellowship pilot circled the campsite known as "Palm Beach" and reported that the missionaries' small plane with all the fabric stripped off sat alone on the sand. There were no signs of the men.

*Wednesday, January 11:* With authorities notified and a full-scale search underway, the MAF pilot radioed back that he had spotted one body. Later that afternoon, another.

By the time the ground party reached the site on Friday, it was too late for their help. The devastating truth was discovered that all five missionaries were dead—slain by the same men whom they had hoped to win to Christ.

Bodies? Is this how a great 20th-century missionary adventure ends? Unfinished? With dead men floating in the murky waters of a strange South American river? From our perspective many years later, we see that, far from being the end of a great adventure, it was merely the beginning. Today, hundreds of Aucas have acknowledged Jesus Christ as their Lord, including some of the same men who spilled the blood of five young servants of God.

This incident graphically reminds us that it is the sovereign God who decides who finishes a given task. As His agents of change, many times we are called to the ministry of beginning, with completion left for those who follow.

## Facing the Consequences

Moses knew for years that he would never lead Israel across the Jordan River. At the waters of Meribah (Num. 20:2-13), Moses and Aaron both forfeited their right to enter the Promised Land. So what did Moses do? Get mad and quit? He kept right on leading, faithfully, as God had called him to do. The fact that the final triumph would not be part of his experience didn't keep Moses from continuing to serve God. Moses pleaded with God a final time (Deut. 4:21-29) to let him cross the Jordan, but accepted the divine verdict and named a successor to lead Israel into Canaan.

It is also significant that there is no trace of bitterness in Moses toward God for this decision. Moses could have reasoned: "After all I've done for You, this is what I get? I stood before Pharaoh, delivered the people from Egypt, put my own life on the line in prayer before You to secure their pardon when they rebelled, tramped around with them for an extra 40 years, and this is what I get? Thanks a lot!"

But we see none of that. Moses teaches us a much-needed lesson in accepting the consequences of our own behavior, and going on from there.

Solomon, in his wisdom, wrote: "A man's own folly ruins his life, yet his heart rages against the Lord" (Prov. 19:3).

As God's agents of change, we are not given some type of spiritual diplomatic immunity against suffering the consequences of our own actions. Yet as the above verse notes, after making a mistake or deliberately disobeying, we somehow manage to get mad at God for what has happened.

The forgiveness of God is unfathomable and complete; yet God does not automatically cancel out the consequences of our actions. It is possible that some wrong thing we do may short-circuit our opportunity to complete a task. We may be forgiven, but excluded from further participation in a given arena of change.

This does not mean that we are useless to God, nor does it cancel our responsibility to remain faithful to the opportunities He does give us to serve Him. We can be assured that even the consequences of our failures are pliable in the hands of our heavenly Father and can be used for our best (Rom. 8:28).

## Unfinished Business

As God's agents of change, the consummation of our life's vision may also elude us through no fault of our own. Much of our lives may be spent in building foundations for others.

On March 13, 1930, a 24-year-old assistant at the Lowell Observatory in Flagstaff, Arizona startled the world with the discovery of the ninth planet in our solar system. Clyde Tombaugh went down in history as the man who discovered Pluto.

But Tombaugh could never have done what he did without the work of astronomer Percival Lowell, who died in 1916. Back in 1905, Lowell predicted the location of a new planet, based on his observations of an unknown force of gravity which was affecting the orbits of Neptune and Uranus. Lowell searched for the new planet for 11 years and died without finding it.

The photographs on which Clyde Tombaugh discovered Pluto were made following Lowell's predictions. One man laid the foundation, and another had the opportunity to build on it.

Near the end of his life, King David expressed his great disappointment that his dream of building a temple for God would never be realized. He told Solomon, "My son, I had it in my heart to build a house for the name of the Lord my God. But this word of the Lord came to me . . . 'You are not to build a house for My name' " (1 Chron. 22:7-8).

The desire of David's heart was thwarted. Yet he went ahead and gathered the materials so that Solomon could begin the project when he took the throne. "I have taken great pains to provide for the temple of the Lord a hundred thousand talents of gold, a million talents of silver, quantities of bronze and iron too great to be weighed, and wood and stone" (1 Chron. 22:14).

The Apostle Paul noted that his ministry of change included preparing the way for someone else. "By the grace God has given me, I laid a foundation as an expert builder, and someone else is building on it" (1 Cor. 3:10).

The entire ministry of John the Baptist was one of preparation. He was an advance man who knew that he would fade out of the picture when the Messiah came. And John used an interesting metaphor to describe his feelings about his role: "The bride belongs to the bridegroom. The friend who attends the bridegroom waits and listens for him, and is full of joy when he hears the bridegroom's voice. That joy is mine, and it is now complete. He must become greater; I must become less" (John 3:29-30).

Complete joy at being the best man and not the groom? Happy to go home alone while your best friend walks away with the bride? Satisfied with just getting things ready for someone else? These are strange sounds to ears that have been told that early birds get the worms and victors get the spoils. But John the Baptist found complete joy in his role, even though in a real sense, completion as we often understand it was never part of its design. And we should not end our consideration of John the Baptist without noting that Jesus said of this "advance man": "I tell you the truth: Among those born of women there has not risen anyone greater than John the Baptist" (Matt. 11:11).

As Christian agents of change, we must remember that we have been called to cooperation with God, not necessarily completion. We are called to be faithful, even if the fulfillment of our vision is not included. We are called to glorify God, not simply to get things finished.

This reasoning is not an excuse for shoddy work or for not finishing a job because of inadequate planning. It simply reminds us that in our work of change, we may not be permitted to finish everything we start.

## Spiritual Navigating

The writer of the Book of Hebrews likens our life to the running of a race and issues this challenge:

> Therefore, since we are surrounded by such a great cloud of witnesses, let us throw off everything that hinders and the sin that so easily cntangles, and let us run with perseverance the

race marked out for us. Let us fix our eyes on Jesus, the Author and Perfecter of our faith, who for the joy set before Him endured the cross, scorning its shame, and sat down at the right hand of the throne of God. Consider Him who endured such opposition from sinful men, so that you will not grow weary and lose heart (Heb. 12:1-3).

An image created by this passage which has persisted in my mind for many years is that of runners on an oval track straining toward the finish line while thousands of people seated in a large stadium cheer them on. I believe that this is a valid picture and one that had meaning to the original recipients of this letter. Symbolically, the witnesses are those Christians who have gone on before us, the heroes of the faith mentioned in Hebrews 11, who now observe our progress in the race assigned to us.

But a consideration of several modern sports has given me a new understanding of the race which involves us as Christian agents of change. The sport of orienteering requires the competitor to both traverse a cross-country course and navigate with a compass and a contour map at the same time. Certain checkpoints must be passed, reaffirming the charge to use correct methods on the way to the correct goal.

The object in orienteering is to move as quickly as possible without losing your bearings. Just as in our role as change agents, speed is unimportant if we're moving in the wrong direction.

Our race as God's agents of change is not always neatly marked by white lines like the lanes on a running track. Rather, we face the prospect many times of navigating through rough country, where alertness and vigilance are essential. It is a race "marked out for us" (Heb. 12:1). But in the tangle of difficult circumstances, the boundaries become more obscure and the apparent shortcuts more inviting.

The finish line in our race cannot be seen from the starting point. For all practical purposes, the finish line is unmarked. We never know where it is. It could be just over the next hill or around the bend. We're not told to fix our eyes on the finish line, but on our Coach, the Lord Jesus Christ.

During the television broadcast of the 1980 Winter Olympic Games from Lake Placid, New York, millions of people were surprised to learn that in the cross-country ski races, the coaches were allowed on the course. From time to time, we would see a man or woman carrying a stopwatch and a clipboard, running alongside a skier, shouting instructions and encouragement. It's a reassuring picture because our Coach is not sitting on a bench with His arms folded, waiting to see how we do. In the person of the Holy Spirit, He is on the course with us, encouraging us, giving instruction.

The race we run, as we work for spiritual change, is a distance run and not a sprint. We are instructed to run with perseverance and are reminded of the process through which God develops the qualities of character and hope in our lives. It is a race which requires training and discipline to run successfully.

## Our Relay Race

Not long ago I sat in the home of a prominent physician who is a medical genius. After a short time in practice, he turned to research and development of medical products to meet the specific needs of suffering patients. That evening, he showed me his latest development—a type of "artificial skin" designed to aid in the recovery of people who had suffered severe skin wounds or burns. It was remarkable.

As I drove away that night, I felt discouraged. It seemed that in light of his accomplishments, my own life was counting for very little. But I was encouraged by these words: "I have brought You glory on earth by completing the work You gave Me to do" (John 17:4).

The thought that liberated my spirit and encouraged me was the realization that I don't have to complete the work God has given this gifted doctor to do. I'm responsible to finish what God has given *me* to do. It may seem like a small thing to realize, but it has revolutionized my attitude since then.

Our race as God's change agents is a relay race. We are not the first to run, nor are we the last. Like those who prepare the way for others and who build foundations, we are charged with faithfully running our leg of the race, and then passing the baton to the person who will continue after we are through. As God's agents of change, we do not function as lone rangers, but as members of the body of Christ on this earth. Everything we do and how we do it affects the performance of the whole team.

When we become weary and tempted to quit, we are to consider the only One to run a perfect race—Jesus Christ. When we are misunderstood, we should remember that some people judged His acts of mercy and healing as proceeding out of an alliance with the devil himself. When we suffer unjust punishment, we need to recall the lashes and the crown of thorns He received for a perfect life of goodness. And when we move toward vengeance and retaliation, let us not forget that the One who could have called 12 legions of angels to His defense did not even answer the false charges of His accusers.

When He had given His life as the price paid to set us free from the oppression of sin, Jesus said, "It is finished." It was not a cry of despair from a man who wanted to hang on and do more, but a victor's cry of triumph, given as He won the ultimate victory over sin and death.

But how could Jesus say, "It is finished," when there were so many blind men left to heal, so many lepers left to cure, and so many hungry left to feed? In His great prayer to God on behalf of Himself and His disciples, Jesus said: "I have brought You glory on earth by completing the work You gave Me to do" (John 17:4). God expects nothing more and nothing less from us than He did from His own Son.

What is the work God has given you to do? Where has He given you the task of functioning as His agent of change? In a classroom, in the cab of a truck, in a large university, at home with your children, in a wheelchair, a nursing home, a pulpit, a bank? The key to being used by God is to run the race He has marked out for you and do the work He has given you to do.

## Crossing the Finish Line

I have seen death close at hand and yet it remains a mystery to me. My own death seems as remote as a distant planet, yet it is a reality more certain than tomorrow. When my moment of death arrives, it is sure to come with mixed feelings. There is the desire to join my Saviour in a life far superior to this one. Yet there are the ties of this world which are not easily loosened.

My desire is that in spite of all that remains unfinished, God may grant that same sense of completeness to me which Paul must have known as he said: "I have fought the good fight, I have finished the race, I have kept the faith" (2 Tim. 4:7).

As God's agents of change, He calls us to prepare the way for others, to build foundations, to run faithfully in the race marked out for us, and to cross a finish line known only to our heavenly Father. It may appear that the visions of our life are left unfulfilled, the dreams of our hearts only partially realized, and the tapestry of the changes we sought, woven incompletely.

Yet we must remember that we have been called to this partnership with the Almighty and have been required only to be faithful. We follow a Saviour who was struck down in His prime, yet knew the approval of God on the completsd mission of His life.

Change it? Turn it around? Make the situations and companions of our lives somehow different and better for the kingdom of God? Yes, that is our calling as ambassadors of a God who seeks reconciliation with His unfaithful human creation. It is a calling that requires us to see and feel the hurt of a dying world and say,

Change it, Lord.

And You can begin with me.

## STUDY QUESTIONS

1. "God's finish line for our lives may be much closer or much farther away than we imagine." How does this statement affect your thinking about your life and your role as an agent of spiritual change?

2. What does it mean to "complete the work which God has given you to do?" How can you know if you have done this?

3. What are some characteristics of a relay race that compare with our work toward spiritual change?

4. List what you believe are the key elements in the work which God wants you to do.

5. Without being morbid or overly sentimental about it, try writing a brief eulogy which you would want others to say of you at your funeral.